A005195

This book is to be returned on or before
the last date stamped below.

WOMEN'S PERSPECTIVES ON DRUGS AND ALCOHOL

For my daughters Emily and Lucy

Women's Perspectives on Drugs and Alcohol

The vicious circle

PAMELA RAINE
Lancaster University

Ashgate

Aldershot • Burlington USA • Singapore • Sydney

Published by
Ashgate Publishing Limited
Gower House
Croft Road
Aldershot
Hampshire GU11 3HR
England

Ashgate Publishing Company
131 Main Street
Burlington, VT 05401-5600 USA

Ashgate website: http://www.ashgate.com

British Library Cataloguing in Publication Data
Raine, Pamela
    Women's perspectives on drugs and alcohol : the vicious
    circle
    1.Women - Drug use 2.Women - Alcohol use 3.Women alcoholics
    - Services for 4.Narcotics addicts - Services for
    I.Title
    362.2'9'082

Library of Congress Control Number: 00-107884

ISBN 0 7546 1429 8

Printed in Great Britain by Antony Rowe Ltd., Chippenham, Wiltshire

Contents

Foreword

In the field of alcohol and drug use, gender has been traditionally defined as society's expectation concerning behaviour viewed as appropriate for members of each sex. A fuller notion of gender as both a process and an institution has been absent. For example, as a process, gender is a part of all human interactions and shapes the meaning of 'female' and 'male' and 'masculinity' and 'femininity' on cultural, political and economical levels. Here, gender has an effect on the social groupings of men and women and divisions between both the private and public arenas of social life.

As an institution, gender is a part of culture just like other components of culture such as symbols, language, norms, values and so on. It is a stable form of structured inequality and embedded in culture. In this context, gender is a normative and moralising system that exerts social control on all in society. Gender brings to society a set of inter-related norms centred on the activities of individuals. These individuals are marked by differences on the basis of being 'male' and 'female' as well as 'masculine' and 'feminine'.

Women who experience alcohol and drug problems go through a variety of problems of daily living by the very fact that these substances are embedded in their lives. Their lives are full of many obstacles both privately and publicly and these lives are riddled with shame. Furthermore, social expectations of these problems *and* the experiences of these problems are gendered.

In this book, *Women's Perspectives on Drugs and Alcohol: The Vicious Circle*, Pamela Raine recognises the centrality of gender and gender relationships. She goes beyond the traditional view of gender that has been put forward in this field. She recognises the complexities of gender as a process and an institution and appreciates the subtle and often hidden, unexpected ways that gender infiltrates the lives of women drug and alcohol users.

On a theoretical level, Pamela Raine introduces refreshing, new ideas into a field where women have been traditionally the underdogs. She offers a thorough and thought-provoking account of women's problematic experiences with alcohol and drugs. Consciously, she allows the voices of women to come through. In turn, these voices are contextualised by key themes drawn from compelling narratives. For example, these substances

vi

created chaos in the lives of these female substance users, while complex mechanisms of social control shaped their gendered experiences of these substances. Help-seeking responses of professionals and the advantages and disadvantages of treatment are contextualised as key areas in these gendered experiences. In the end, the author makes far-reaching recommendations that match the results of this important research.

We learn how gender influences the ways in which users co-ordinate their space, their time, their substances, community resources, and others (whether those others be other users, relatives, families, carers). This is a rich account and a welcomed piece of research in a field which urgently needs gender sensitive work.

Elizabeth Ettorre
Professor of Sociology
University of Plymouth

Acknowledgements

I would like to thank the following people and institutions for their help during the writing of this book: Keith Soothill and Carole Truman, my PhD supervisors, for their constructive criticisms, encouragement, and belief in my abilities throughout the research process; Roger Clough for his input in the early stages of the study; my postgraduate colleagues in Applied Social Science, particularly those with whom I shared room space, Lisa Bostock and Schuichi Ito; Veronica Holmes and Mary Toder for their practical help and unfailing cheerfulness; all the staff in the alcohol and drug agencies I visited for their time and patience, particularly Tony Ryan from Turning Point, Manchester; the women who took part in my study who generously shared their stories with me; my parents for their support and childminding, without whom I would have been unable to continue; and my daughters Emily and Lucy who have borne the brunt of my lapses in parental attention over the past few years. Particular thanks go to Elizabeth Ettorre, of the University of Plymouth, for her kindness and encouragement, and for writing the foreword to this book.

Thanks also to the Economic and Social Research Council, who funded the research on which this book is based from October 1996 to March 1999.

Introduction: Women on the Margins

...all women share the social predicament which can lead to problems with drugs. It could be me, or you, or any woman, who experiences such problems. (Sargent, 1992, p4)

This book explores a number of questions concerning women's problem drug use and drinking. It details findings from research which examined the type of problems women experience in relation to drinking and drug use; sought to determine how, why, and by whom a woman's substance use becomes identified as a problem; and to consider what happens when women seek help for their problems. A central argument of this book is that the cultural, social, and economic inequalities women experience *as women* are crucial to an understanding of their drinking and drug taking. As its title suggests, the main focus of the book is on women's personal experiences of drug use and problem drinking.

As a means of setting the discussion in a wider context, however, I look first at feminist critiques concerning welfare provision for women, and how these relate to alcohol and drug services.

Alcohol and Drug Services for Women in the Context of Health

Contemporary feminist debates concerning the impact of health care on women are characterised by their diversity. Common themes, however, include the controlling, repressive aspects of medical practices and relationships in interactions with women, and male control of the health profession at the highest levels (Pascall, 1997). Traditionally, women's roles are rooted in the private sphere of the family, providing care for others; both dependent on a male provider, and having others - children, the elderly and the sick - dependent upon them. As providers of informal care, therefore, they are placed in a particular relation to health care providers in the public sphere. Their interactions with health professionals may, for example, be affected by stereotypical assumptions on the part of doctors as to what constitutes women's role in society, and what is appropriate behaviour for women (Ettorre and Riska, 1995). Furthermore, imbalances of power between doctor and female patient frequently influence such exchanges (Barrett and Roberts, 1978; Roberts, 1985); negatively affecting women's ability to negotiate from positions of strength (Dobash, Dobash and Cavanagh, 1985). The medical profession has been criticised, therefore, for exerting undue control over women's lives, particularly in relation to reproduction and fertility control.

The type of criticisms levelled by feminists at health care services in general find their echo in debates concerning treatment provision for women with alcohol and drug problems. The extent to which feminist critiques have influenced service development in what is primarily a 'male preserve', that is alcohol and drug agencies, is however, questionable. Problems emerging from alcohol and drug use are seen as primarily affecting men; therefore both research and service development have concentrated, in the main, on male interests, with the result that:

> The lack of a body of knowledge about women and substance abuse led those, specifically psychiatrists and psychologists working in the field, to assume that substance use was primarily a 'man's disease' or a 'male problem'. (Ettorre, 1989a, p594)

Professional responses to women's substance use are criticised as being based on the needs of the male as the 'normal' drug taker; while research into alcohol and drug problems and service orientation also tends to be geared towards the needs of men (Reed, 1987; Ettorre, 1992). Furthermore, professionals in the substance abuse field, and academics conducting research are predominantly male. This gender imbalance affects what are seen as legitimate topics for study, how the research is carried out, and what is considered important in informing service development. Women's interests are marginalised; because they fall outside the 'standard white male' pattern of substance use, they are seen as 'doubly deviant', both as women whose behaviour falls outside the norm for their sex, and as drug users and drinkers (Reed, 1987, p153).

In addition to the perceived male bias of research and treatment traditionally the main focus of attention concerning use of mind-altering substances has been medical and psychological (Gabe, 1991; Ettorre, 1992). This model, by emphasising individual dysfunction, takes little account of the social and economic situation of women and how this influences their use of alcohol or drugs. As Marsh (1982) points out, 'Efforts to study situational factors - social, economic and cultural, related to drug use have been relatively few' (p159). She describes the medical model as 'one in which people are not held responsible for either the cause of their problems or the solution'. From this perspective substance misusers are 'victims of a disease' who require expert intervention in order to effect a 'cure' (p155). While medicalization of an issue has the advantage of reducing the stigma and blame experienced by the user, it also affects the nature of responses and inhibits the understanding of other factors.

Although the psychological approach to substance use is important in understanding the motivation of the individual user, it is limited in its application. For example, studies that focus only on individual psychology tend to imply solutions at an individual level. The type of rehabilitation policies applied to alcohol and drug users, following the logic of this model, operate to maintain the status quo, by returning the user to 'normal' functioning. Social problems are therefore defined in terms of defects of the individual, and wider issues, such as gender power relations, and the effects these have on patterns of alcohol and drug consumption, are not addressed (Sargent, 1992).

Sociologists researching drug and alcohol use, particularly feminist sociologists, have challenged the supremacy of the psychological, medical, and individualist approach. Ettorre (1992), for example, argues for a 'critical approach which views substance use as a complex social issue with specific political implications, rather than as an epidemiological concern (that is, as an individual disease, a psychiatric disorder, or even an implicit moral failing)' (p5). If substance use is examined in its social context the debate can be moved from the image of the individual as 'wilfully perverse' towards an account rooted in women's daily lives (Perry, 1979).

During the last twenty years or so the masculinist approach to drinking and drug use has been challenged by an expanding body of work which addresses women's specific concerns. Until relatively recently, however, 'the situations and needs of women were largely unacknowledged and recognised within both the treatment and research world' (Ettorre, 1992, p17). The primary intention of my research, and this book, therefore, is to contribute to an understanding of women's substance use from a feminist sociological perspective.

Current Trends in Service Provision

Service provision in the UK for those with alcohol and drug problems is currently an eclectic mix of statutory, voluntary and self-help initiatives. A major change in recent years, however, is the shift of policy emphasis to providing care in the community, in a move away from the traditional view of treatment as a hospital based activity. Alcohol treatment units and drug dependency units, usually attached to psychiatric hospitals, were established in most areas of the UK during the 1960s, providing services such as detoxification, group psychotherapy, occupational therapy and individual counselling. Alongside the closure of large psychiatric hospitals some units have also closed, however, while others have become community based agencies (Harrison, Guy and Sivyer, 1996).

The *Treatment and Rehabilitation* report from the Advisory Council on the Misuse of Drugs (ACMD) in 1982 focused on the provision of services at a local and district level. In the north-west region of the UK the aim was to set up a community drug team in each district, to work alongside general psychiatric services (Strang, 1989). In this respect the north-west was ahead of the field in regionally organised service development for drug users. Community alcohol and drug teams are now the main form of local statutory service; these usually consist of multidisciplinary teams of two or three full-time workers (typically a community psychiatric nurse and a social worker, often with a consultant psychiatrist and nursing services attached). Treatment on offer will vary, but will usually include individual counselling, and often some form of group therapy. In response to the threat of AIDS, during the 1980s needle exchange schemes for injecting drug users were expanded (MacGregor, 1989). Within the NHS the majority of recent treatment initiatives, therefore, have been aimed at outpatients.

In the wake of the *Tackling Drugs Misuse* report (Home Office, 1986) extra funds were provided by central government for the provision of new services, taken up by both statutory and increasingly, voluntary organisations (MacGregor, 1989). Projects have been variously funded by the Home Office, health authorities, local authorities, and through joint funding arrangements. The role of the voluntary sector in alcohol and drug provision is an expanding one, particularly in offering advice and counselling, crisis intervention, and longer term rehabilitation. 'Street' agencies, such as the Lifeline Project in Manchester, have often been at the forefront of service innovation (Strang, 1989). Residential rehabilitation units are for the most part provided through the voluntary sector, although the private sector now plays an increasing role (Harrison *et al.*, 1996).

Changes in service provision in recent years, however, have meant a reduction in the number of residential places available for substance misusers, since the implementation of the NHS and Community Care Act (1990) in April 1993 moved responsibility for funding from the Department of Social Security to local authorities. It is as yet unclear what the long term effects of these changes will be on alcohol and drug services in general, and specialist services for women in particular. Financial stringencies, however, do tend to have a negative effect on the provision of specialist women's services (Ettorre, 1997).

Feminist Alternatives

Differences in perspective amongst feminists necessarily affect perceived 'solutions' in respect of women and health care. Radical feminists, for example, in the 1960s and 1970s campaigned for women-only forms of health provision, intended to empower women to take control of their own health, and provide *alternatives* to state welfare (Williams, 1989), while others placed the emphasis on reforms within existing services. Early feminist activists in the field of alcohol and drug provision, for example the Women's Group of the Camberwell Council on Alcoholism and the Drugs, Alcohol, Women, Nationally (DAWN) group, found difficulties both in attracting funding and in influencing mainstream policy debates; although their influence at grassroots level was arguably more far-reaching (Thom, 1994). Finding favour for separatist women's services is problematic, in a policy climate that favours improving generic services, and which sees radical feminist demands as representing marginal interests. Some success was enjoyed, however, by DAWN, for example, in influencing such government funded groups as Alcohol Concern and the Health Education Authority to take women's service needs seriously (Thom, 1994). As a result of their campaigns agencies such as the West Cumbria Women's Project (an agency participating in my study), serving predominantly female clients, were established.

In relation to self-help for female alcohol and drug users, existing organisations such as Alcoholics Anonymous and Narcotics Anonymous provide group support, using the 'twelve step' approach. For those who find this clinical (and often male-dominated) approach unhelpful other support groups (some for women only) have become established, mainly in the voluntary sector (although a number are run by community drug teams) (Doyal, 1995). The majority of women seeking help for their alcohol and drug problems, however, are obliged to use mainstream services in the absence of other alternatives.

Structure of the Book

The first chapter of this book sets the scene by reviewing the current state of knowledge regarding women's drug and alcohol problems, while in Chapter Five, I review research concerning women's underuse of drug and alcohol treatment services. The remainder of the book is based on the findings of my study of twenty-three women drug users and problem drinkers (seventeen of whom were resident in drug and alcohol rehabilitation units). My study was set up to explore such questions as whether there are aspects of developing alcohol and drug problems which are specific to women, and if so, how such problems are related to their life situations. I looked at how, why, and by whom women's drug use and drinking is problematised, and how significant others in their lives influence problem recognition and formal help-seeking. Finally I considered the question of what happens when women seek treatment, in their interactions with health professionals, and in residential rehabilitation.

The study sample falls broadly into two main groups; younger women (aged 35 and under) who primarily use illegal drugs, or are chaotic drinkers and occasional drug users; and older women (aged over 35) who are primarily problem drinkers. Ten senior alcohol and drug treatment agency staff, from both the statutory and the voluntary sector, also participated in my study, and their views are represented in this book. Details of the research design are outlined in Appendix One, while further characteristics of the sample may be found in Appendix Two.

In Chapter One of the book I review research which sets women's drinking and drug use into its social context, covering topics such as women's caring responsibilities, paid work, social change, social support, social stress, and experiences of victimisation. Social evaluations of women's drinking and drug use, and the consequences of such judgements for women, are also included in this chapter.

Chapter Two explores chaotic elements of women's lives associated with their drinking and drug use. Firstly, the physical and psychological effects are described, including both positive and negative aspects. The major part of the chapter, however, is concerned with identifying those aspects of chaos which are specific to women - that is histories of violent victimisation, self harm, and the lifestyle consequences of alcohol and drug use.

In apparent contrast to the previous chapter, Chapter Three focuses on the experience of control in alcohol and drug using women's lives. In common with the chapter on chaos, however, it focuses on the gendered dimensions of these experiences. For example, women's perspectives on control are discussed; firstly concerning the role played by drugs or alcohol in coping with everyday life, that is in 'getting by'; and secondly the control exerted by women in 'getting straight' (drug and alcohol free). Both these aspects of control are related to women's social situations. In this chapter other facets of control over women's lives are also discussed; these include external controls - the 'double standard'; family responses to women; and responses by male partners (the principal agents of control over women). However women are not merely the passive recipients of control by others; for example they engage in 'bargaining' with partners and resistance to controls; strategies which are detailed in the latter part of this chapter.

The main topic in the fourth chapter is the influence of significant others (including family members, friends and male partners) on women's problem recognition and help-seeking. As male partners are seen as important influences on women's behaviour I consider the ways in which they affect women's help-seeking, and examine the strategies which they typically employ in resisting change. Theories developed concerning domestic violence are used to further understanding of the nature of heterosexual relationships which include drug use or problem drinking. Concepts of privacy and boundary control, for example, are used to illustrate how women's problem recognition and subsequent help-seeking may be influenced by the dynamics of intimate relationships.

From Chapter Five onwards the focus of the book changes to women's under-use of alcohol and drug treatment services, reviewing current knowledge concerning the barriers to formal help-seeking for women. Factors relating specifically to alcohol and drug treatment services are explored; these include professional attitudes towards women who misuse drugs and alcohol, access to treatment services, service orientation, and service options open to women.

Chapter Six further considers responses by health professionals to women who use alcohol and drugs problematically, in the light of my study. This chapter includes such issues as communication between women and their doctors, access to specialist treatment, professional attitudes towards prescribing alternative medication, and women's experiences of hospitalisation.

In Chapter Seven I examine the costs and benefits of treatment for women in residential drug and alcohol rehabilitation. The benefits of treatment described by women study participants include increased self esteem and independence, improved social support systems, and feeling safe. The costs of treatment are identified as primarily concerning access to childcare and minority status in treatment; for example in terms of relationships with male service users, mixed groupwork, communal living and 'gendered space' in agencies. Also included in this chapter are strategies for reconciling the benefits and costs of treatment for women, for example prior screening for physical and sexual abuse. The chapter concludes with a consideration of the case for separatist treatment for women.

In the final chapter I draw together the threads of the arguments presented in this book, stressing the gendered dimensions of women's experiences of drug use and drinking. Differences between women are as important, however, as their commonalties; the key differences between women study participants are therefore described (doubtless there are others, but they are outside the scope of this book). Finally, I offer some thoughts on policy regarding alcohol and drug provision for women, and touch on potential changes in the wider social sphere, which are important not only to female drinkers and drug users, but to all women.

A Note on Terminology

This book is concerned with women's use of any chemical substance, including alcohol, 'that alters mood, perception or consciousness *and/or* is seen to be misused to the apparent detriment of society and the individual' (Ettorre, 1992, p7).

The literature concerning drug or alcohol use employs a number of terms such as 'addiction', 'abuse' and 'drug dependency' to identify the field of interest. Definitions of these terms vary according to the approach of the researcher or practitioner, and at times seem interchangeable. I wish to make it clear, therefore, that this book is concerned with women experiencing *problem* drug or alcohol use, which according to the Advisory Council on the Misuse of Drugs (ACMD) (1982) includes:

> ...any person who experiences social, psychological, physical or legal problems related to intoxication and/or regular excessive consumption and/or dependence as a consequence of his (sic) own use of drugs or other chemical substances. (in Griffiths and Pearson, 1988, p20)

Although this definition includes physical or psychological dependency as a *possible* consequence of drug taking, it need not necessarily be present for problems to exist. The distinction between problem drug taking and dependency or addiction is, in any case, a subjective matter. It is probably more useful to see drug and alcohol use on a continuum ranging from occasional use, through regular recreational use to dependency; this should not, however, be seen in any way as an inevitable progress, as the habits of an individual are subject to fluctuation.

1 Women's Drug Use and Drinking in Context

Introduction

In this chapter I consider those aspects of women's lives which are of crucial importance to an understanding of their drinking and drug use. These fall into two main areas; firstly the social organisation of society, which defines women's relationships to men in both the public and private spheres; and secondly the cultural norms and values which underpin this gendered organisation (Bograd, 1988; Ussher, 1998). Gendered social organisation affects women's life chances and opportunities, and includes economic factors, educational and employment opportunities, housing, protection from violence and abuse, the availability of legal and emotional support, the material consequences of marriage, and the presence of children (Ussher, 1998); while cultural norms affect perceptions of drug use and drinking, and responses to women who engage in such behaviour. *It is not only what women do which constitutes the problem, therefore, but the social and material conditions in which they do it.*

The concept of the 'gender order', which is described as a socially constructed set of power relations between women and men, in which men as a group wield the greater power (Connell, 1987), provides a useful theoretical framework within which to examine the meaning of problem drug use and drinking for women. While acknowledging that, from a feminist perspective, 'material factors often mitigate against women: women are often economically, physically and socially disadvantaged in relation to men' (Ussher, 1998, p153), the concept also embraces the possibility of change and transformation.

Each topic in this review touches on the social, cultural and material influences on women; including caring responsibilities, paid work, social support, social stress, and experiences of victimisation. The *consequences* of substance use for women are also inevitably linked to ideological factors; therefore social evaluations of women's alcohol and drug use are discussed. Women's experiences and social circumstances differ, and change over time,

9

however; changes which may be the result of individual and collective struggle (Connell, 1987).

In the discussion which follows I shall consider how what women do, the circumstances in which they do it, the opportunities open to them, and the expectations which bind them, affect their drug use and drinking.

Drug Use and Problem Drinking in Context

The Unseen Costs of Caring

Providing care for others traditionally falls on women; they are largely responsible for the day-to-day care of children and elderly, sick or disabled relatives. Although the state accepts some part of the task through social and education services, caring work in the family is largely taken for granted, unpaid and unremarked, and performed, in the main, by women (Ussher, 1991). Land and Rose (1985) refer to this phenomenon as 'compulsory altruism' for housewives, around which state services are built and on which the state depends. The problem for women resides in the responsibilities attached to such caring work and the circumstances in which it takes place. For example, the cost for the carer may be exacted in terms of stress, loss of independence, financial hardship or dependence on the state, social costs such as isolation and curtailment of other relationships, and in some cases physical and mental health problems.

Studies have connected women's drug use to coping with the circumstances of caring. It is not, it is argued, that women are simply more willing to complain of illness, as suggested by sex-role theory, but that the nature of the work affects their health negatively (Graham, 1993). Ettorre and Riska (1993), for example, describe how some women use psychoactive drugs as a resource in the management of everyday life. Drug taking can be seen in this context as a form of 'passive resistance' or 'taking something for themselves' (Ettorre, 1992, p140), or simply as a means of surviving.

Alcohol may be also used to relieve stress associated with caring for others, as an example from Betsy Thom's study demonstrates:

> Coping with her mother's pain and distress, with her own lack of sleep and with the pressure of running home from work to care for her mother has made this respondent turn more and more to alcohol which she described as 'a medicine to my mind'. (Thom, 1986, p784)

Similarly, evidence from a study by Davis (1994) in the United States, which compared women who completed drug treatment to those who drop out, demonstrates that many women use drugs to 'stay well'. If these women were deprived of drugs 'they often could not get up in the morning or carry on with any of their daily activities, including caring for their children' (p1300). In prioritising their children's welfare women who use drugs reflect the attitudes of women in general (Taylor, 1993).

Paid Work: The Benefits and Costs for Women

Paid work emerges from research as an important resource for women, for example in providing some protection against stress (Pascall, 1986). However the nature and conditions of work, in combination with other responsibilities carried by women, can serve to weaken this protective factor. Alcohol consumption is higher amongst employed and professional women (Colten and Marsh, 1984; Waterson, 1996), while in many cases women need to combine employment with childcare, which creates its own problems and balancing of responsibilities. Reed (1985), for example, describes the complexities of paid employment as a resource for women:

> ...most women juggle multiple roles. The consequences of these multiple roles appear to be related to whether the women has chosen the roles or felt compelled to assume them. For some women, family roles protect them from job-related stressors, or vice versa. For other women, movement into the workforce creates stress and more use of chemicals. Women's job opportunities are often very limited and low paying, with little opportunity for advancement. (Reed, 1985, p34)

Some women attempt to cope with these diverse elements by 'trying to be superwomen who do it all - an effort doomed to failure' (Johnson, 1982, p113). The types of stresses experienced by women in work documented by Johnson include the type of employment available, particularly if it is low-paid, temporary or part-time. Women may also experience problems in the workplace, including discrimination and sexual harassment. The balance between the supportive effects of work and negative, stressful influences, largely depends on these factors, and how they are experienced by the individual. There is evidence, for example, that women involved in alcohol and drug treatment generally enjoy less in the way of economic resources than men (Reed, 1985). Furthermore, they rarely anticipate the prospect of full-time employment on completion of rehabilitation (Marsh and Miller, 1985).

Social Change and Diversity

Life for women has been changing in different ways. For example, more women now have children outside marriage, and rates of divorce and remarriage have increased dramatically over the last few decades. Women are living in more diverse circumstances than was the case in the immediate post-war period, when the nuclear family was the conventional arrangement.

The impact of changing employment rates for women is also important, as the number of married women taking up paid employment outside the home has steadily increased since the 1950s (Reed, 1985; Graham, 1993). Since the manufacturing industry has declined in this country, however, the type of work available to women tends to be concentrated in the service sector, and is less likely to be full-time and permanent. Financial strain has become an increasingly common fact of life for many women, as economic recession has affected either their own or their partner's work prospects (Belle, 1982). The type of pressures and insecurity engendered by these various factors may lead some women to find relief in drugs or alcohol, or both (cf. Wolfson and Murray, 1986).

Problems with alcohol or drugs may also appear at different life stages for women. A study by Wilsnack and Wilsnack (1991), for example, concerning the epidemiology of alcohol use, points out that women in the younger age group (aged 21-34) are most likely to develop problem drinking, but also most likely to move out of it because of various events (e.g. motherhood, change of job, change of partner), while *chronic* problem drinking is most common in an older age group (aged 35-49). Both social change and individual life changes may therefore impact on women's substance misuse.

Social Support: Relationships

Those elements of women's lives which provide a supportive social structure may include relationships with partners, children, and wider kin and friendship networks, in addition to work colleagues. Social support has been described as 'a key ingredient in both physical and psychological health' (Ussher, 1998, p160). The *lack* of a close relationship with a husband or partner emerges strongly as a factor in the lives of women experiencing alcohol and drug problems (Marsh and Miller, 1985; Gabe and Thorogood, 1986; Reed, 1987; Smith, 1992a).

The influence of significant others on women's lives, however, is also noted as a factor in beginning and maintaining alcohol and/or drug use.

Women with drink problems, for example, are often married to men who are heavy drinkers, and may experience marital problems (Orford, 1985; Estep, 1987; Forth-Finegan, 1992). A common type of experience is described in Thom's study of women entering treatment for alcohol problems.

> Being a good wife sometimes meant participating in a husband's leisure pursuits, sharing his friends and being seen to 'fit in' to his way of life including his drinking habits. (Thom, 1986, p782)

Women with male partners, therefore, may not experience their relationships as supportive. This is a topic which I explore in detail in a later chapter, as although existing research identifies substance using partners as potentially negative influences on women's initiation into and continuation of alcohol and drug use the underlying processes are not as yet fully explored.

Social isolation may be an increasing difficulty for some women, as women's social networks are often smaller than men's (Reed, 1985). The consequences for the individual are occasionally severe, as one heroin user in Sargent's study explained:

> I started using more [heroin] because I was feeling lonely, and that is a very important thing. I think it's one of the main reasons why people start using it - because everyone's living so apart from one another. (Sargent, 1992, p83)

Evidence suggests, however, that the nature and quality of women's personal networks is important, rather than the simple fact of their existence (cf. Davis, 1994), in instigating and maintaining substance use.

Research suggests, therefore, that women who develop and maintain problems with alcohol and/or drugs may experience deficiencies in their informal interpersonal networks. It is also noted that men are less supportive of female partners who have problems with alcohol or drugs than when the situation is reversed, and marital problems and divorce are common amongst this group (Reed, 1985).

Social Stress and Material Resources

The causes of stress are many and various; they may include 'life events, chronic difficulties, cultural change or lack of change, and changing concepts of role in society. Stress can also result from the individual perceiving loss, failure or deprivation' (Women's National Commission, 1988, p34). Stress can be experienced in connection with a specific event, such as bereavement, a partner's or child's ill-health, spouse's unemployment, or with an ongoing problematic social situation; for example, poverty, poor housing, experiencing long-term health problems, or caring for a child or sick relative (Thom, 1986). Amongst working-class women in particular, vulnerability to physical and psychological problems may be increased by their material circumstances, such as low income, poor housing, lack of amenities and the fear of violence (Brown and Harris, 1978; Miles, 1981; Belle, 1982; Sluka, 1989; Payne, 1991). Such women are also more likely to be divorced than women from higher socio-economic groups, with the accompanying risk of economic disadvantage. Becoming a single parent, the majority of whom are women, is also to be more vulnerable to reliance on state benefits, which equates to a poor standard of living (Graham, 1993). A study in the United States of 43 low-income families in diverse circumstances, for example, which tested the relationship between life situations and mental health, concluded that:

> Much of the stress in life comes not from the necessity of adjusting to sporadic change, but from steady, unchanging (or slowly changing) oppressive conditions which must be endured daily. (Makosky, 1982)

Other feminist commentators point out that women's traditionally subordinate position within families reinforces their lack of control over income and resources (Payne, 1991). If women are not in paid work, for example, in some households their husbands may control family finances.

Use of mind-altering drugs may be a means of coping with a life crisis or a stressful situation. In Thom's study, for example, of women in alcohol treatment, 'while most men talked of alcohol consumption causing them problems women still spoke largely in terms of other problems causing them to drink' (1986, p993). Drug use and drinking, in this context, can be seen as a method, albeit potentially destructive in the long term, of coming to terms with the unalterable.

Problematic drinking is commonly connected with psychological distress, in particular with depressive illness; for example, women in treatment for alcohol and drug problems report high rates of depression (Harrison, 1989). To some degree, depression can be seen as a more 'natural' response to stress for women than drinking to excess or taking drugs, as it does not carry the same social stigma.

Research into the effects of stressful social circumstances on health, according to Payne (1991) underestimate the effects on women. This is because the type of stress inventories frequently used to assess stress levels in individuals commonly overlook vital elements of women's lives; for example the isolation of housework, the oppressive nature of some aspects of women's social roles, and the discrimination commonly experienced by women. Payne argues that these material aspects of women's lives are given little or no weight in much stress-related health research.

The type of social stress described here may be encountered almost routinely in women's lives. While social stress theory does not imply that all women, or even the majority of women, will react to these events or life circumstances by use of psychoactive substances, it does attempt to explain why some respond in this way. For some women, however, the experiences which precipitate alcohol and drug problems are more traumatic.

Experiences of Victimisation[1]

> Rape, domestic violence, and other victimisations are far more common in the experience of chemically-dependent women compared to other women in their communities. (Blume, 1990, p298)

The theme of victimisation recurs throughout the literature on women's drug use. The association of experiences of abuse in childhood, for example, with the development of alcohol and drug problems in adulthood has been noted in numerous studies (e.g. Miller and Downs, 1993, 1995; Miller, Downs and Testa, 1993; Ireland and Widom, 1994; Downs and Miller, 1996). In a report to the Women's National Commission (1988), for example, Betsy Thom stated that 'many women who become addicted to heroin have experienced disruption, poor parental relationships and often violence and drug abuse in their families' (p82). In Miller and her colleagues' (1987) study, women in an 'alcoholic' sample, in comparison to a control group, were significantly more likely to have experienced sexual abuse as children. Furthermore, the total number of instances of abuse experienced by the women was greater, and the abuse had lasted significantly longer than for women without alcohol problems. In reports of a later study Miller and Downs (1993, 1995) suggest that childhood victimisation may lead to feelings of low self esteem, which alcohol use helps to ameliorate; or alternatively the feeling of 'difference' on the part of victims may encourage them to join deviant peer groups in which alcohol and drug use is socially acceptable.

Women in alcohol and drug treatment also report physical and sexual victimisation as adults. A study by Ladwig and Anderson (1989) of women substance users in prison, for example, found that 19.7% had experienced sexual abuse, and 27% reported some form of sexual or physical abuse prior to imprisonment. Harrison's (1989) study in the United States of 572 women from 21 treatment centres also discovered high levels of physical abuse by male partners, particularly amongst the under 35 age group. Drug use or drinking, for women in these circumstances, may be interpreted as a strategy for coping with the intolerable; a means of dulling a painful reality.

In studies of parental abuse towards children the majority of research, with the exception of Miller and Downs' work in the United States, fails to control for the gender of the abusing parent. Miller and Downs (1993) suggest, therefore, that the contribution of adult male perpetrators to the development of women's alcohol problems should be considered in future studies of the long-term effects of victimisation.

Social Evaluations and Consequences

> ...women are, in part, the way they are because of the way they are thought to be. (Oakley, 1974, p1)

In addition to the type of social stresses routinely experienced by women, social evaluations of women's drug taking and problem drinking behaviour tend to be more negative than for men in similar circumstances. Reed (1985) argues that this is because 'different standards of judgement' are applied to men and women (p28). The relative acceptability of minor tranquilliser use by women (related to passivity, valued in women), compared to alcohol (associated with loss of control) reinforces this viewpoint.

Public concern about women's drug use tends to focus on their role as 'moral guardians' of the family and ignore the structural constraints on women 'behaving well'. Despite changing rates of involvement in paid work for married women, societal judgements concerning behaviour still relate to what is seen as their primary domestic role (Gomberg, 1982). In this respect little has changed for women since this comment was made by Child, Barry and Bacon in 1965:

> Under the generally prevailing conditions of human life, temporary incapacity of a women is more threatening than temporary incapacity of a man. For example, care of a field can be postponed for a day, but care of a child cannot. The general social role makes drunkenness more threatening in women than men. (quoted in Gomberg, 1982, p13)

Women who do step outside what is seen as 'acceptable' behaviour for their sex may suffer more severe societal reactions than men, particularly if they have children in their care. There is a subtext which reads as follows:

> The real underlying message for a woman is that, at all times, she should be in control of herself, mindful of her spouse, her children, her responsibilities and her work situation. If she feels strung out, stressed, unable to cope, she should avoid mind-altering substances. (Ettorre, 1992, p77)

Although there may be some evidence of a relaxation in attitudes towards women's social drinking in general, this does not extend to *approval* of problem drinking. Negative repercussions of alcohol consumption were experienced to a greater extent, for example, by the younger women in Gomberg's (1988) study, which compared 'alcoholic' and 'non-alcoholic' women's attitudes towards male and female drinking, although the younger women themselves were more relaxed in their attitudes to drinking. These repercussions took the form of more criticism and less communication with parents, quarrels with family members, and rifts with friends. Possible explanations for this age-related discrepancy could relate to the greater public visibility of younger women's drinking, or to their being of childbearing age. A drunken woman is seen as 'a bad mother, uncaring for her children, or an irresponsible wife, not considering the needs of her husband' (Ettorre, 1992, p39). A more relaxed attitude may be taken towards drinking in older women, who, while lacking the power and status of their male counterparts, may nevertheless enjoy greater social tolerance than young women. Illegal drug users are, however, in the words of one heroin user, 'subjected to more nastiness from society' (Sargent, 1992, p7). Such nastiness may manifest itself in legal repercussions including imprisonment, removal of children into care, and controlling the supply of methadone, clean needles and condoms.

Social reactions to women's drinking contain an element of moral disapproval. Heavy drinking and drug use are associated with promiscuity and prostitution in women, an association which seems to be based more on hearsay than on hard evidence (Gomberg, 1982; Ettorre, 1992). Those drinking or drug using women who do not conform to the 'norm' for their sex of monogamous heterosexuality; lesbian women, for example, or single mothers, may be particularly vulnerable to moral censure.

Conclusions

Women's drug use and drinking takes place, both private and publicly, in a context in which women occupy a subordinate space. A feminist materialist approach to substance use focuses on the social, economic, and material influences on women, and women's responses to these factors. Intimate relationships (particularly with a partner), social networks, and work opportunities are all significant factors in women's lives, which can provide valuable protection against stress, or act as life constraints. Ettorre (1994a) points out that, 'It could be argued that women, as strategic actors, choose to use substances as a way of adjusting or modifying their behaviour in response to their oppressive social situations' (p97).

Sources of stress, which women may respond to by drinking heavily or using drugs, may include traumatic events, or more routine everyday problems involving caring responsibilities, chronic ill-health, and unequal access to material resources such as income, housing and social amenities. Responding to such stresses by drinking heavily or using drugs, however, for women, is certain to attract negative judgements from others. Alcohol and drug misuse therefore tends to push women further towards the 'periphery of social power' (Ettorre, 1992, p141) and adds to their vulnerability to stress-related problems, in a type of vicious circle. Part of this vicious circle may involve experiences of sexual and/or physical abuse, in the majority of cases perpetrated by men.

In the following chapter, using examples from my study, I explain how for many women drinkers and drug users becoming entrapped in the vicious circle may tip over into chaos.

Note

[1] I am aware of the problematic nature of the term 'victimisation', from a feminist perspective, used in relation to abuse suffered by women. However I use the term in Kirkwood's sense as referring to a *process*, rather than attaching the label of 'victim' to a particular woman. As she points out, '...women are often simultaneously victimised and actively surviving' (1993, p137).

2 Drugs, Alcohol, and Surviving Chaos

Introduction

Throughout my study, while listening to women drinkers' and drug users' accounts of their lives, I was frequently struck by the severity of their problems. These were often deeply traumatic and disturbing, and could, in certain respects, be described as chaotic. While I should stress that I am not suggesting that chaos is an inevitable aspect of everyday life for such women, chaotic experiences were a common feature of many drinking and drug using women's stories. This chapter is an attempt to convey something of their experiences.

Part of the remit of my research was to consider how women's experiences of alcohol and drug problems relate to their life situations, to the 'concrete reality of women's lives'. Throughout this chapter, therefore, I consider gendered dimensions of chaos; that is the way in which certain experiences, in particular histories of violent victimisation, self-harm, and the lifestyle consequences of alcohol and drug use, are affected by gender. I begin, however, with a description of the often severe physical and psychological effects of alcohol and drug misuse.

Drugs and Alcohol: The Physical and Psychological Effects

It would not do justice to the women in my study simply to focus on the negative aspects of their stories, as from some accounts it was possible to understand the attractions of a drug using lifestyle. Indeed a number of younger women were anxious to impress on me the reasons why they had come to rely upon mind-altering drugs. They emphasised the initial pleasurable effects of using, and the importance of the social element of drug taking and drinking; which could be described as the 'rewards' of the lifestyle (Davis, 1994). For example:

> There were so many people in the flat all the time, and there was, oh, drugs for man and dog. But at the time it was like, 'I'm having a good time, I'm partying!' Got into the smack [heroin].
>
> So immediately as soon as the speed [amphetamine] came round it was, 'I'll have a bit of that'. Whereas most people start off swallowing it and snorting it, but not me. The Christmas of '89, that's when it came to a head. I was getting right out of my head, all the time. But I suppose if you're enjoying it...I started to get right into the smack [heroin] as well, and I loved it like. It's a dangerous drug that, thoroughly loved it. (Emily, aged 28)

For some women the attractions of taking drugs were described in almost emotional terms, as Chelsea explained:

> I do try to explain it's [heroin] like a lover; you need it, you want it, and if it's took away from you miss it. (Chelsea, aged 21)

Subsequently, however, the negative physical and psychological effects of heavy drinking or drug using began to emerge in women's lives, diminishing the initial pleasurable aspects. Two women, for example, described the physical consequences they experienced:

> I think because I've had one addiction or another, over the years, while I was a chronic amphetamine user. I should point out that I had two habits over that period. There was lots of morphine sulphate about. It was just something to hit up, basically. But withdrawal I had from that, a lot of bad pain in my kidneys, aching all over, feeling sick. I was in a really bad way. (Bev, aged 35)
>
> So I was sort of hopeless, lying on the couch just in and out of consciousness, dirty, being sick, runs, just coming out both ends, couldn't eat at all, my blood pressure was sky high and I was having panic attacks all the time. They just came and took me to hospital. (Lucy, aged 33)

The psychological effects of alcohol and drug use were a major factor in continued use, however. One young woman clearly described the daily physical and psychological battle with herself involved in coping with her heroin habit.

> I was taking it every night, and I didn't have the willpower not to take it. And once I got addicted it's a vicious circle. I needed it; I couldn't do without it. I couldn't last more than an hour or so; it was the

withdrawals. And the mental thing - the good bit tells you not to, and the bad bit says, 'Oh go on'. (Emma, aged 24)

When the stage was reached where obtaining the desired substance became the only meaningful activity in life; caught up in the 'vicious circle' some women became careless about exactly what they were taking, with potentially disastrous consequences. For example:

> Then one night a mate of ours came bouncing in, he could hardly stand up. To see him in such a state, was, 'That must be good gear [heroin], eh?' I wasn't ready for the strength of the gear, and I had a hit of it and I just went...crawling on my hands and knees. It's like you...when I was eight years old and got my first pair of glasses, the world looked like that. You couldn't focus, whatever. I managed to crawl back into my room and I had a roomful of people and I just went - out like, and they went out. And I cannot account for the next twelve hours, I just woke up in a pool of vomit like. How I survived that I do not know. By rights I should have died that night. (Emily, aged 28)

As my study progressed I became acutely aware that the women I was interviewing were the *survivors* of alcohol and drug abuse. Their experiences, however, require placing in the context of other events in their lives, in order to explain how they became enmeshed in such situations, and how they attempted to cope with them. This context is one in which gender plays a crucial role.

Violent Victimisation

> I have come across it round here, that the guy is the master in the household; the woman drinks in the afternoon, he comes home, finds her drunk, and beats seven bells out of her. There's still a lot of violence attached to this, the macho ideal; the woman is there to do what they want, and that's an end to it. (Community alcohol and drugs team leader, male)

Research evidence suggests links between childhood victimisation and the subsequent development of alcohol and drug problems amongst women (see for example, Miller *et al.*, 1993; Ireland and Widom, 1994; Miller and Downs, 1995, 1996), and between sexual assault in adulthood and the subsequent abuse of alcohol and drugs (Burnam *et al.*, 1988). Recent research in the United States found significantly higher rates of severe violence from either parent were recounted by women in alcohol treatment programmes (65%) than by women in households (38%) (Miller and Downs, 1993). The authors suggest, therefore, that there may be links between the development of alcohol problems and experiences of violent victimisation.

> ...the experiences of childhood victimisation may result in feelings of low self-esteem, which may lead to women using alcohol as a way of coping with negative feelings about themselves. (Miller and Downs, 1993, p142)

It is also argued that women who suffered abuse in childhood continue the pattern as adults; that is abused children grow up to be abused women.

The majority of women taking part in my study had histories of physical, sexual or emotional abuse. Two women had been physical abused as children, for example, and eleven as adults (ten of the latter by their male partners), while five women had been sexually abused as children and five as adults. In addition three women reported experiencing instances of verbal or emotional abuse from partners, while one woman described being sexually harassed at work. In total 15 women (65% of the sample) reported at least one abusive incident in their lives, while for women in residential treatment the situation was bleaker still; of 17 women in treatment, 13 had histories of abuse (76%).

Instances of abuse may be *underreported* in these interviews, however, as women were not directly questioned on the subject, but volunteered the information without prompting. Those women in this study who did disclose abusive incidents had often been repeatedly victimised, as the following examples illustrate.

Jenny, a problem drinker, for example, when describing her childhood and her relationship with her father, explained:

> He loved me in his own way. My dad liked wee [small] lasses, and his daughter was one of them, unfortunately. (Jenny, aged 49)

In addition to a sexually abusive relationship with her father, Jenny had also experienced a turbulent relationship with her mother, who 'battered' her with a stick throughout her childhood, and on occasion during her adult life. Subsequently her husband was frequently violent towards her, culminating in her being thrown out of the family home (without her children). For many years Jenny had felt unable to discuss the abuse she had suffered as a child, and at the time of interview she was obviously still very distressed by the memory.

Chelsea, a young heroin user, had similar experiences of sexual abuse as a child. She attributed her drug use to these early experiences, and her father's refusal when confronted to acknowledge that anything untoward had taken place between them. His continued denials in the face of her accusations led her to doubt the truth of her own memories of events. She told me:

> It's like I got abused when I was a child, when I was nine years old, and I hadn't had a lot of love and affection from my dad as well. I was quite frightened of my dad really because it was my dad that did it...he put it all on me. I resent him a lot for that and I suppose for not getting the love and affection; I think that's probably why I have gone onto drugs. People have just not listened to me. I've probably got the attention from drugs, which you do, you get what you need from drugs, you get the good feeling. (Chelsea, aged 21)

The pattern of abuse had continued throughout Chelsea's adult life, with violent assaults by her long-term male partner. She explained the nature of her relationship with him; it was:

> A bad relationship in a way, a violent one. He always used to say, 'I haven't hit you or anything', but he used to batter me all the time, because if you can't get your drugs you stress don't you? It's my fault that he can't score, it's his fault if I can't score, you know.

> ...it was just when we both got onto heroin, it was as soon as he got into heroin he changed into a completely different person. He's had a knife up to my throat and everything, he's knocked me senseless; he broke my nose, kidnapped me for a weekend and what have you. So I suppose from being an early age I've just got used to it, and that's why I do not trust men at all. (Chelsea, aged 21)

Chelsea's experiences were typical of those of the young drug using women in my study, for whom casual violence from their partners was an unexceptional part of everyday life. Their tolerance of such abuse was often, although not invariably, connected with their need to maintain a regular supply of drugs through their male partners; to the extent that it was a 'normal' feature of such relationships.

In another example Lucy, a drinker and occasional drug user, had endured severe physical and sexual violence from men. Shortly after the birth of her youngest child she was raped by strangers, and her two long-term male partners had also subjected her to extreme violence. In addition to beating her on a regular basis her most recent partner had also attacked her baby daughter. She explained:

> ...the children's father was putting blades to my throat, smashing the place up, black eyes and just threatening me and just really awful. He was hanging the baby out of the window threatening to throw her out; he went to punch me and punched the baby in the face. She never even opened her eyes; she was only five weeks [old]. (Lucy, aged 33)

Throughout these often horrific attacks on herself and her child Lucy did not press criminal charges against her partner. Although her account represents an extreme example of the type of physical and sexual violence experienced by women in the study, it was by no means an isolated incident.

Sadly, some relationships which had begun hopefully, and were seen as a means of escape from previous bad experiences, later proved to be abusive in nature. Anne Marie explained, for example, how her marriage initially seemed a welcome sanctuary after a childhood spent in local authority care. However, the benefits were short-lived.

> I'd been married for about five years. To a really horrible man. And I just walked out and left him one day with the children. And I never went back. He used to beat me up. I wasn't allowed to have any friends. I'd no washer, no Hoover. It was hell on earth. All my hopes and dreams of getting away from my childhood and all that was all banished when he came on the scene. (Anne Marie, aged 41)

When women were involved in long-term abusive relationships they described how their self esteem became gradually eroded, with the result that their ability to change things was reduced (cf. Kirkwood, 1993). A woman's drinking or drug taking behaviour was sometimes used as a justification for violence against her; a justification which could be accepted by the recipient of violence as reasonable (cf. Sargent, 1992; Taylor, 1993). The tendency for women to focus the blame for abuse on themselves has been documented by feminist research involving 'battered' women (Hoff, 1990; Kirkwood, 1993), and women who are married to men who drink problematically (Ussher, 1998).

Women who drink to excess (particularly in public), or who use drugs are already designated as 'unrespectable' by virtue of their lifestyles; in a world where 'individuals get what they deserve and deserve what they get' (Stanko, 1985, p92) being battered by men can be seen as justified. Women may therefore be considered 'fair game' for violence if they drink or take drugs. In my study several women attributed incidents of rape to their own intoxicated state at the time; thus placing the blame for such attacks firmly on themselves. For example:

> I was raped by my friend and that was because I was too drunk to do anything about it; that was through alcohol. That was a family friend of twenty years...that was through drink. (Sue, aged 47)

> And I also ended up getting raped, through the abuse of alcohol. Whereas I wouldn't have got myself in that situation in the first place if I hadn't been drinking. It just leads you into situations, which, in normal life today, you would not dream of doing. You become promiscuous, and you just don't have any respect for yourself. Which causes problems when you're sober, because you feel disgusted with yourself, ashamed. It's a very bad drug. (Anne Marie, aged 41)

These women expected little sympathy from others; they felt they deserved what they got because of their 'bad' behaviour. The additional stigma attached to drinking or drug problems, and women's acute awareness of that stigma, therefore exacerbates the documented tendency for women to self-blame when victimised. In taking the responsibility for their victimisation they were simply following society's example.

There were exceptions in this study to male patterns of violent behaviour, however. Kayleigh (aged 37), for example, described how she became violent towards her husband when she had been drinking; she had outbursts of 'battering' him during joint drinking sessions, although the level of physical damage inflicted during these attacks appears to have been slight. Wilsnack and Wilsnack (1991) explain that:

> Heavy drinking may allow women to express anger that is typically suppressed, and women's heavy drinking is likely to occur in the context of heavy drinking by companions. (Wilsnack and Wilsnack, 1991, p135)

I should emphasise, however, that as my study participants' experiences demonstrate, drinking and drug using women are more often on the receiving end of violence by men. Their susceptibility to violent behaviour and powerlessness in the face of it is exacerbated by their status as 'deviant' women, in addition to which the degree of trauma experienced in these situations may be linked to their degree of powerlessness to effect change (Busfield, 1996). Power imbalances between men and women, and the exercise of power in the form of abuse are therefore important to an understanding of women's substance use. They are also important in appreciating why some women, lacking the resources, do not simply leave abusive situations (Hoff, 1990; Kirkwood, 1993; Ussher, 1998).

Violence towards women has also been linked with increased rates of self-harm and suicide (cf. Doyal, 1999). For a number of women their desperation with their situations was such that they began deliberately harming themselves, threatening suicide, or making (often repeated) suicide attempts.

Self Harm

Women across the spectrum of alcohol and drug users, and from different age groups described self harming. There were differences in the type of self destructive acts, however. Amongst those in the under 35 age group, for example, five women described deliberately cutting themselves. The following examples are typical of this group:

> You've totally got no confidence, no self esteem. You totally think you're worthless, you don't care about yourself at all. I also used to harm myself as well, I used to cut my arms as well because I used to hate myself that much for messing my life up, for being in a state. That was when I was really down, but towards the end it got more and more; it got a lot more frequent towards the end because I just couldn't see a way out of it. I thought I was in a rut and I just couldn't get out of it. I couldn't see a way out of it at all. (Lauren, aged 23)

> That's why I'd scratch my arms, using a pin or something. That's why I've got these scars. I'd punch anything. I'd beat my hands so much they looked like they'd gone septic, all puffy and black. And basically I felt like I was going mad. And it was a case of physical pain temporarily calmed down a lot of the emotion, a lot of what I was going through. I think that was probably the worst time of my life. (Bev, aged 35)

More women in this younger group also reported feeling suicidal (including 'accidental' overdose); five women described these type of feelings compared to two women in the older group (aged over 35). However, a greater number of women in the over 35 age group (predominantly alcohol users) actually carried out suicide attempts; five in this group of women, compared to two in the younger group. The following examples are typical of those women who reported actual suicide attempts:

I got it into my head, if I just got a bottle of Prozac, and just did away with myself that would solve everybody's problems. But I always stopped, just about the last minute - panicked and told somebody. Actually the last time I did it I ended up in the police infirmary. And I was put on the antidote, and my body rejected it. They just about lost me. (Jenny, aged 49)

...prior to that I'd taken about five to six overdoses with alcohol. I've woken up in hospital on a drip a few times; the last one was pretty bad. I nearly died. (Rachel, aged 41)

There would appear to be a fine distinction in some cases between 'accidental' overdose, mixing drugs in what one woman described as 'deadly cocktails', and deliberate self harm, as one woman's experience illustrates:

I'd had about two litres of wine and I asked my sister to come around, to tell her I had a drinking problem and to take Librium. I don't remember anything about it; apparently I fell down two or three times when my sister was there. When I got up in the morning I noticed all the Librium had gone, so I rang my sister to see if she'd taken it away for safe keeping, and she said, 'No, you took it all last night'. (Sue, aged 47)

For some women the final crisis triggering help-seeking was quite simply a matter of personal survival, such was the overwhelming nature of their despair. For example:

I needed help. I'd just given up, lost. It's hard to describe, it's just...I thought I'd either go into rehab. again or die. That was it. I would have done it. (Lucy, aged 33)

They can't help me, nobody can help me, I've had it. And that's when it can get very dangerous. Because the last twelve months, that's when I started not caring what I was taking. I wasn't purposely going out to kill myself, but I wouldn't have cared if I didn't wake up. I couldn't have cared less, like. (Emily, aged 28)

The risk attached to their behaviour for these women posed a real threat to their lives. Previous studies have linked increased risk of suicide with excessive alcohol use amongst women (see Plant, 1997 for a review). Such risk-taking behaviour is also common amongst illicit drug users (Harrison, 1989; Sargent, 1992), in what could be described as 'gambling with death' (Morrice, 1976). Self harm and self destructive behaviour may be perceived as an expression of conflict and has been linked by commentators to previous experiences of physical or sexual abuse (Hoff, 1990; Koss, 1990). Deliberate self harm in response to such abuse can therefore be seen as a gendered phenomenon, commentators suggesting that it is twice as common among women as men (Gormon, 1992).

Self harm may also be 'time out' for women, and permit 'the ability to survive amid a state of chaos' (James, 1997, p13). It may also give the powerless a sense of control over their lives, which is otherwise lacking (Doyal, 1995). Paradoxically, therefore, although self harm can be seen as a destructive response to abusive incidents, it can also, alongside substance use, be perceived as a form of coping, albeit a negative one. As Hoff explains:

> ...suicide, assault, addictions, and emotional disturbances *are* forms of coping, though most people would regard them as unhealthy or ineffective. (Hoff, 1990, p73)

A spectrum of self damaging behaviour can be identified; from initial experimentation with alcohol and drug use, to regular and harmful use, compulsive use, accidental overdose, deliberate self harm, to the final stage - suicide attempts. The rate of progress through the stages of harm is not an even one; it is more rapid, for example amongst the younger group of alcohol and polydrug users. Nor is it an inevitable process. The more chaotic the women's lives became, however, the more risky their activities tended to be, in a type of downward spiral.

Lifestyle Consequences and Stressful Events

As women became more heavily engaged in drinking or drug taking their lives tended to become increasingly chaotic, as gradually they began to lose contact with 'straight' [non substance using] people and became embroiled in a lifestyle in which drinking or taking drugs was simply an accepted part of life.

The consequences of chaotic lifestyles, particularly for drug users, involved frequent casualties. Witnessing drug overdoses and occasionally the deaths of fellow users was particularly traumatic, as two women's experiences graphically illustrate:

> He [friend] pushed the speed over to me, and he was getting more and more smack. The night he died, he said, 'I'm going for some gear [heroin], are you interested?' I said, 'Aye, but keep it quiet, I'll come

down to you'. Later on that night when W. [husband] had gone home, B. [friend] didn't answer the door. I all but kicked the door in, shouting, 'Let me in you bastard, you're taking my gear'. He was dead. Next morning they're carrying him out in a plastic bag, like. (Emily, aged 28)

I've been in a flat where somebody's been on the floor, and I've said, 'Who's that?', and they've said, 'It's just such and such a person'. I've gone over and they've actually been dead and people were just walking over them, waiting 'till it gets dark so they can take them out, and things like that. I thought I was quite streetwise before I took heroin, but it opened my eyes a lot, it really did. Just the lifestyle really and knowing that it was just getting worse and worse. (Lauren, aged 23)

Lauren explained that her awareness of her situation had become dulled with repetition and the effects of the drugs. What to others would be horrific events could be viewed by women involved in the lifestyle in an almost fatalistic manner.

...when you're on gear [heroin] you don't realise what harm you're doing. You don't realise how dangerous it is, and what a horrible lifestyle you're leading because it becomes normal to you, everything you do, people dying, climbing over dead bodies. It just becomes normal to you. (Lauren, aged 23)

Although Lauren had believed at first that she would escape the worst effects of drugs the sheer unpredictability of events and 'a lot of people dying', particularly the death of her best friend, brought it home to her that she was vulnerable. She also realised that if she were in difficulties she could expect little help from those for whom such casualties were a 'normal' part of life. Shared experiences with alcohol or drugs were the focus of group life, often to the exclusion of other activities and other people.

It would be a case of smoking, crashing out, waking up, smoking again, crashing out; you'd have fag burns all over the quilt because that's what you did. (Joanne, aged 28)

Ironically, within superficially social drug using circles women users could become socially isolated, detached from any useful sources of help and support by their dependency (Rhoads, 1983). Three women described, for example, how their drug use began as a social activity, shared with groups of friends, or in large gatherings, such as acid house parties. Over time, however, the social element of their activities diminished, as drugs began to take a greater hold, and the importance of friendships dwindled. Some women recognised that they were sharing their lives with others through necessity and convenience, not because of genuine friendship or sympathy. For example:

> Well if they can stick a needle in your arm they're not friends are they? Nobody knows really how to inject do they? They just see a vein and they go for it or whatever, and if someone could put a needle...and something could go wrong, then it just says it all really. (Chelsea, aged 21)

As many women are initiated into drug use through their male partners it is also often the case that they take on his friends, becoming part of his social circle as a consequence (Rosenbaum, 1981). In addition, Parker and his colleagues' research into drug use in the Wirral area (Parker, Bakx and Newcombe, 1988) noted that as women became more involved in the 'smack' [heroin] scene they were more likely than men to become detached from old friends; this was because a greater number of male friendships were with other drug users.

There were instances where women in the study had attempted to break away from what they recognised as destructive influences, only to discover that their previous friendships had weakened or effectively disappeared. As one woman explained:

> I got arrested for stealing cars I think after that, I got fined and I got arrested again. I was that frightened of going to prison that I stopped hanging about with him [boyfriend], but by this time I knew that many people that were on it [heroin], it was like a case of who isn't on it? (Lauren, aged 23)

In a 'catch 22' type of situation the more women became entangled in scoring and taking drugs, and caught up in the lifestyle, the more difficult it became to escape. The more horrific the events unfolding, the more drugs were required to blot out reality, in an escalating spiral of chaos. While drug use may have initially been a type of coping mechanism in dealing with stressful events, its effects were in fact to increase social isolation and stress (Rhoads, 1983).

Women's less extensive social networks may decrease their ability to cope with stressful situations (Reed, 1985). The tendency therefore for female substance users to experience less social support than their male counterparts increases 'maladaptive coping mechanisms', such as drug use and self-harm (Rhoads, 1983).

Conclusions

In this chapter I have described the chaotic nature of many female drug and alcohol users' lives. Physically and psychologically the toll on these women was heavy. Drug and alcohol abuse, and its effects, however, do not exist in a social vacuum; gender is a crucial dimension affecting both its antecedents and its consequences. For some women violent assault had preceded the development of problems with alcohol and drugs, while for others it was an integral part of the lifestyle. Research which takes women substance users as its focus has touched on their histories of physical and sexual violence (for example, Thom, 1986, 1987; Sargent, 1992; Smith, 1992; Taylor, 1993); however violent victimisation has not been central to the analysis. As a consequence the importance of sexual and physical abuse as a precursor to drug use or problem drinking, I would suggest, has not as yet been fully understood.

The extent to which women in this study suffered from physical, sexual and emotional abuse is appalling to contemplate: some of their stories were harrowing in the extreme, as I hope this chapter has illustrated. It was the interweaving of histories of abuse, however, with other aspects of women's lives which made their situations so traumatic. In addition to suffering the physical and psychological effects of alcohol and drug use, and physical or sexual victimisation, for example, many women had harmed themselves, or attempted suicide. Self-harm has been linked by researchers with previous experiences of abuse and powerlessness in personal relationships; as a means of coping with the stress and anger generated by such experiences, or as a means of surviving amongst chaos. While drug use can be similarly seen as a coping mechanism, for these women it had become part of the problem.

As a consequence of the lifestyles associated with heavy drinking or drug use, including adopting their partners' social circles, many women had effectively become isolated from supportive networks; friendships had become disrupted and family ties weakened. These are major factors in entrapping women in circumstances in which choices narrow and chaotic experiences become a 'normal' part of everyday life.

Two aspects of chaos emerge as particularly important in understanding the issues which confront women substance users; firstly the ways in which gendered inequalities contribute towards chaotic events in problem drinking and drug using women's lives; and secondly the interconnections between factors such as victimisation, self harm and the lifestyle consequences of alcohol and drug use, in their impact on women's physical and mental health, their engagement in society, and ultimately their survival.

3 Controlling Women

Introduction

Although chaos is an ever present threat in the lives of many women drug users and problem drinkers, it coexists with its apparent opposite - control. Whether relating to self control, or more often control by others (particularly men), this theme is one which frequently recurs in women's stories, either overtly, or as an unspoken subtext.

The belief in the disruptive effects of drug use on society stems from the idea that 'self-control is the key to the orderly flow of social life' (Ettorre and Riska, 1995, p115), and that 'hedonistic addiction runs counter to the ethos of a disciplinary society' (Smart, 1984, p34). Historically, social concern in relation to drug use in general, and women's drug use in particular, appears most in evidence at times of social and economic change (Waterson, 1996). At a time of increasing independence, socially and economically, for some women, coupled somewhat uneasily with a renewed emphasis on women's primary role in maintaining the moral health of the family, conflict at both a personal and political level is perhaps inevitable. This conflict can be perceived, perhaps in its most stark forms, in the lives of female alcohol and drug users.

Because women are key players in maintaining an orderly society and in social reproduction, the strictures placed on them to avoid behaviour perceived as destructive, such as heavy drinking or drug taking, are more severe than those commonly imposed on men. Sargent (1992), for example, argues that:

> Freely permitted individual pleasure through drugs and/or sexual activity, *especially in women*, can be seen as a threat to the economic and political stability of the state. (Sargent, 1992, p12-13, emphasis in original)

Such threats are dealt with in part by the application of controls, both internal and external, on the lives of women. Paradoxically the theme of control appears both in women's use of mind-altering substances to cope with everyday life, that is 'getting by'; and in their attempts to control such use by 'getting straight', that is alcohol and drug free. Dimensions of control affecting women also include external controls - the pervasive societal 'double standard', family reactions, and responses by partners to alcohol and drug use. Individual men have been identified by previous research as the primary agents of control over women; control which is perhaps best understood by perceiving it as a continuum - at one end of the spectrum as an expression of love and caring; at the other as stigmatisation and repression (Holmila, 1991). However, women are not merely the passive 'victims' of controlling practices by others; they are active agents in negotiating the terms of the 'bargains' which they strike with male partners, for example. In this chapter I consider in detail how this bargaining is played out between women alcohol and drug users and their male partners, and the type of resistance tactics employed by women in challenging the gendered balance of power.

'Getting By': Using Alcohol and Drugs to Cope with Life

It appears contradictory to describe using alcohol and drugs to maintain a semblance of control over events; substances more usually associated with being 'out of control'. For example cultural representations of drug use perceive the user as:

> ...someone whose life is controlled, if not ruled or governed totally, by drug taking. Hence, the drug user is not in control of his or her life; the drugs have taken over control. (Ettorre and Riska, 1995, p115)

A number of women in my study, however, used alcohol and drugs as a means of coping with everyday life, and remaining in control of events. In one example, Adele, a heroin user, explained her usual strategy for maintaining her daily routines. Typically she would buy a week's supply of heroin at a time, and split it into seven portions; one for each day of the week. She said:

> I'd always have something in the day. Make sure I'd saved something, so I could have something that morning. I've got two [children] now but I only had one then. I'd always make sure I had something so I could get up and see to her. I'd get up a bit earlier, smoke my drugs, and just carry on with my day. (Adele, aged 26)

Using drugs, according to Adele, helped her to deal with her normal domestic routine. If she was without heroin she explained, 'I couldn't be bothered to do anything. I'd try not to put myself in that position, I'd always make sure I had something'. Similarly she would take drugs before going to work, so that her performance would not be affected. Another drug user, Lauren, also described her typical daily regime:

> I worked in ..., but it was just really hard, because like at dinner time I'd have to run to the chemist, get my methadone. When I took my methadone in the morning it had worn off by dinner time, so just before they called you off for your dinner I was starting to feel dead weak and exhausted, and then I'd have to go and score at dinner time, come back, and then it would be the same about four o'clock. I'd start feeling ill again; I did need some more. (Lauren, aged 23)

The importance of keeping up appearances *despite* alcohol or drug use was emphasised by a number of women in my study. Marjorie, for example, explained that although drinking heavily she still took care of her housework; her standards were not allowed to slip. She said:

> For all my binges, I still got up in the morning, had a bath, did my hair. I might not get dressed; I'd clean the bathroom, hoover up and that. I don't like my house in a mess. Even when I've been on real bad benders, that's still been done. Anyone could walk in and the place would be spotless. (Marjorie, aged 43)

Alcohol or drugs were frequently used to counterbalance stress and everyday problems, as an aid to relaxation, or a type of 'medication'. For example:

> When I'm feeling down, it's just a case of using it [alcohol] to try and feel better for a little while. If I drink enough then I forget, so it's not quite as bad. It's like I'm using it as a sort of medication. (Edna, aged 34)

While the motivation for initial drug use was predominantly the pursuit of a pleasurable drug 'high' (cf. Taylor, 1993), this tended to change over time to the numbing of undesirable feelings and emotions. As Joanne explained:

> Well at first like I took it [heroin] to have that buzz, but after a bit you do take it so you're not thinking about stuff; it blocks all your worries out, it blocks your feelings out and your emotions. And that's why when you do your turkey you start crying a lot, because all your emotions are coming back and that. So think about the stuff I had to think about, like any problems I had, I mean I had a habit, I were taking it anyway. But you

> don't think about, when you're taking it you're not thinking about other things, 'cause you're too busy thinking about the drug. Do you understand what I mean? (Joanne, aged 28)

Alcohol could also be used to dull physical as well as emotional pain, as Anne Marie's experience illustrates:

> It [alcohol] just became a crutch, really. It came where I couldn't do without it. At first it was just a crutch, to get me out of my problems, a confidence booster. Pain - to stop pain. Painkillers didn't seem to be that effective. (Anne Marie, aged 41)

For a number of women, the stage was reached where even minor problems required a 'hit' of drugs, to painlessly smooth over difficulties, at least temporarily.

> ...it gets to the point where any little thing that does your head in, something minor you think, 'Oh my God, sack it, I need some gear [heroin]'; then you'll take it and then you're not bothered, it doesn't bother you at all. (Lauren, aged 23)

Using drugs or alcohol as a strategy for remaining in control of life, however, was not unproblematic, and this was recognised by a number of women in the study. The 'vicious circle' they described was that taking substances to relieve their initial problems then led to greater problems, more drug taking and so on. One aspect of their lives which particularly concerned women with dependent children was remaining in control of their children's welfare, despite alcohol and drug use. They were acutely conscious that drug use and drinking do not equate, in the eyes of society, with 'good' mothering (Waterson, 1996). A service provider interviewed in the study pointed out that, contrary to received wisdom, it is not inevitable that drug using mothers, for example, make inadequate or neglectful parents (see also Taylor, 1993). For women involved, however, the nagging fear was that their substance use would get out of control and negatively affect their ability to care for their children. Several women described, for example, the strategies they employed to minimize harm to their children.

> I'd always make sure my little boy was in bed; he sleeps all night. I knew he was safe in his bedroom, and the door was shut so he couldn't get out. He couldn't hurt himself in there; there was nothing to hurt him. (Ali, aged 20)

> I didn't drink through the day because I had a baby and school, but of a night time that's when it...[increased], or probably weekends where somebody else could look after her, my partner you know. (Kayleigh, aged 37)

Adele, a heroin user, similarly attempted to control her drug use in such a way that her mothering abilities, in her opinion, were largely unaffected. In such a way she was able to maintain her habit for a number of years before problems began to emerge.

> It didn't become a problem for a good few years, because I always seemed to have had the money for it. I wasn't an overuser, twenty-four hours a day. I'd use in the morning, then after half-past three, when D [partner] was at home, I'd look after the baby and cook and clean. I never went out, I'd always use in the house. That went on for about four years. I'd only use in the week, not at weekends. (Adele, aged 26)

While attempting to control alcohol or drug use by timing it to fit in with caring or work routines was partially successful, as a strategy it had a tendency to break down in the long term, however. Anne Marie, for example, at first confined her drinking to when her children were asleep in bed. As time went on, however, she began drinking earlier in the day, at around three o'clock in the afternoon, when her children came home from school. Similarly, Mary found that using alcohol, as she saw it, to help her take care of her children, had a negative effect on her actual ability to cope, leading eventually to increased drinking.

> It's a vicious circle. I found it hard to look after the children so I drank, and it got harder to look after the children so I drank more. (Mary, aged 39)

Whether drug use or drinking was seen as a problem by women was often concerned, therefore, with the extent to which it sustained or interfered with daily routines, whether work or domestic. Providing alcohol and drug use was controlled by being confined to appropriate times and places, therefore, it allowed women to continue unchallenged in their public and private roles. Once that control was lost, however, it became increasingly difficult to regain.

When the point was reached where controlling alcohol or drug usage was no longer feasible, women were faced with the prospect of getting 'straight'; that is in attempting to cut down on their consumption or curtail it completely.

'Getting Straight': Controlling a Habit

The majority of women interviewed in my study were struggling either with a harm reduction regime or abstinence, depending on their circumstances. One woman described her feelings about the process, stressing the need to feel in control of her life, as she felt she had been prior to developing a drinking problem.

> When I first got married I didn't drink at all, you know. At the moment I'm trying to take control. I can't control everything. I can't control things that happen, like heart attacks, but I'm trying to retain in my life things that are good for me. And too much drinking isn't part of it. (Helen, aged 48)

Remaining in control of the desire to use substances is a continual struggle for the majority of women problem drinkers and drug users. Gaining control is not a once and for all event, however, but a process involving continual self monitoring and assessment (Holmila, 1991). An amphetamine user in rehabilitation described, for example, the type of fluctuations in mood and motivation she experienced.

> One thing I've found about coming about coming off this stuff is your emotions are all over the place. You're either so incredibly happy it's sickening or you're so depressed that [dramatically] 'Oh, I need to end it all'. You can go from one to the other in half an hour. It's frightening, it really is like. At the moment I'm on top of the world and it's got to mid afternoon and I'm still feeling good, but I'm wary, I'm waiting for it. Yesterday, that was it, I was packing my bags. Sod everybody, I'm off like. It's weird the way it goes. (Emily, aged 28)

For those women undergoing community treatment, maintaining motivation could be equally tough, with the additional problem of keeping up with everyday responsibilities. Anne, a problem drinker, for example, described her progress in recovery:

> I persevered. I slipped a couple of times. But I think this time I'm well on the road to recovery, this time. I've got so much positive attitude now. I can answer back now, when I used to let folk walk all over me. I'll answer back; I won't take no messing off anybody. In fact I was able to take control of me and the kids. (Anne, aged 46)

For Anne, gaining control of her drinking was seen as a first step in controlling aspects of life where she felt she ought to be in charge; that was primarily her family and domestic life. Again, therefore, it was the necessity to care for others which was high on her personal agenda.

Those women who are perceived by others as lacking in *self* control, however, may find themselves subject to controls from other people, as I go on to explain.

The Double Standard: Alive and Kicking?

A popular stereotype of female behaviour insists that women should be seen to be in control of themselves at all times, and in all circumstances. Images of rebellious woman in society are scarce and where they do exist are rarely positive (Holmila, 1991), while images of rebellious mothers are even rarer. The stigma for women associated with alcohol and drug use is therefore doubly damning, as one service provider explained:

> One of the main things is the stigma around abuse [of alcohol], and the stigma of being considered a nurturer, a home keeper; in some areas of society, and by the women themselves, it's considered they should be under control. And to lose control is a double whammy. Not only am I an alcohol and drug user but I don't care for what's going on. (Community alcohol and drugs team leader, male)

The pervasiveness of the double standard for female and male behaviour affects what is seen as appropriate public behaviour for women; reinforced by the prevailing control of public places by men (Green, Hebron and Woodward, 1987). The following experiences are typical of those recounted by women in the study.

> You go into a pub, like, through the day, it might be all right the first time you go in. They might chat to you and buy you a drink. But if you make a regular thing it'll be, 'Bloody hell, she's back in again. Who's looking after her kids? She's going to be in no fit state to mind her kids, she can't look after herself'. But my husband, my second husband, although the first one as well if it comes to that, he could go and play darts or pool, and it's, 'Hiya, do you want a pint, want a beer?' Totally accepted, but for us to do it...but he'd walked away from the kids as well. (Anne, aged 46)

> The amount of times I've heard, I've even heard it in here [rehab.], people say it in here, 'I can't imagine you ever using drugs', and, 'It's not nice when girls stick needles in their arms', but it's all right for lads to do it. I've heard that so many times, and they'll say, 'But you're a girl'; and I'll think, 'So?' (Lauren, aged 23)

Such reactions were frequently encountered by women in the study. It appears that everyone felt that they were entitled to an opinion about their behaviour, and to be able to express it without restraint. Although one respondent suggested that the town in which she lived enjoyed a culture of machismo, which could be responsible for this phenomenon, similar experiences were reported by women from different geographical areas. Women's 'good behaviour' it seems is the responsibility of everyman.

Women themselves were acutely aware of the social reactions to 'out of control' behaviour associated with substance misuse, and to some extent resigned to them (although often considering them outdated) (cf. Gomberg, 1988). The association of such sanctions with childcare and domesticity is strong, because for women public behaviour is inevitably linked to their private, domestic roles. For example:

> Because you're born a female, you're going to be stereotyped; you're going to do this, you're going to do that. Children come along, they're your responsibility. Okay dad's there as well, but mums tend to be the homemaker, don't they? (Helen, aged 48)

> People have a different reaction [to women]. You are the mole that makes the hole, it is different. It affects the family more if the mother, the woman's drinking a lot, I would say. (Brenda, aged 49)

Some men were openly hostile to women drinking in public, for example, as one young, childless woman explained:

> ...going in pubs on your own you feel, well I felt like scum. It's not acceptable. Men will readily say to you, 'You should be at home, you should be doing this, doing that', whereas it's par for the course [for men] going for a few drinks after your tea, before tea, at lunch time.

> *That's still the case is it?*

> Oh yeah. Even in my age group. I think even more so in my age group. It's not the done thing for a woman to be drunk. I'm very aware of it. People I know called me piss head as in - 'I'm nothing but a piss head'.

I've had people steer clear of me because I do drink. I'm known for it and I hate that. And I'm paranoid about going out again. (Audrey, aged 25)

Women may also monitor other women's behaviour in this respect, condemning those who act in an 'unfeminine' manner. Historically, 'women as the moral force of society have been prominent in campaigns in the past against drink and drugs alike' (McDonald, 1994, p22). However the main beneficiaries of such informal constraints are men, as it is their social power which is maintained, constituting a type of patriarchal control by proxy (Green *et al.*, 1987). The divisive nature of such controls prevents women from seeing common elements in their lives which could potentially be a source of mutual strength and support (Hutter and Williams, 1981; Otto, 1981).

The 'double whammy' is also evident in work situations, where men can be allowed more scope for 'behaving badly'. Drinking at lunchtime, for example, may be tolerated in men, whereas it would be unacceptable for working women in similar environments. For example:

> I worked in a large office at Liverpool with people, where it's fine for the men to go out and have a few drinks at lunchtime and then after work, and even coming back into work after a Friday afternoon session. That was just the lads, been out for a drink and that was fine. They'd come back rolling all over the place. But I found when it was myself with a problem I got a very cold reaction. A woman with a drink problem that's bad. A woman who drinks that's just a bad thing. Can't have that at all. An interview I had with my boss for the first time, I had to admit to him I had a problem. It was okay for me to go and get help from my GP, but I wasn't ever to come into work or to ever have a drink around work. I find it difficult to explain what I'm trying to say. I was threatened with immediate dismissal. Whereas I know I've worked with a lot of blokes who've had drink problems, perhaps not to the same degree but they've been *carried* within the workplace and I've heard, 'Joe's been on the ale again'. But for me a woman it was totally not on. (Alice, aged 44)

Although many women in the study rejected the *idea* of other people judging their actions, in some cases they did change their behaviour to avert criticism. Audrey, for example, became increasingly unhappy about being seen drinking in public houses, and Alice was particularly careful to conceal her drinking from work colleagues. Another respondent, Edna (aged 34), explained that because people consider it more shocking for women to be seen drunk, she confined her drinking to her home. Similarly when Emma (aged 24) needed a prescription for methadone she took it to a pharmacy where she was unknown to the staff, in order to avoid social embarrassment. 'I actually purposely went to a chemist a distance away, because the one right next door I didn't want them to know'.

Although these women's personal problems had not diminished they had become less 'visible' and therefore more socially acceptable. It is not only in public, however, that women's behaviour is subject to censure. In the private arena, in particular within the family, informal means of control are also brought to bear on women.

Family Responses to Women's Drinking and Drug Use

The informal policing of women's 'good' behaviour may be carried out by family members and friends of drinkers and drug users. For example:

> They [parents] say I've never been responsible enough. I mean, they know about the drugs at school, I told them about that a long time ago, before any of this came out. And they said, 'I hope you never become a mother, because you'll never be able to look after them [children]'. (Ali, aged 20)

> If I fell out with them [parents] they'd say, 'You smack head, you shouldn't have [your daughter], you're not a fit mother'. (Joanne, aged 28)

A feeling of not being 'good enough', or of not being able to do anything right was common amongst women in the study; feelings which were reinforced by family responses to their substance misuse. Although personal sanctions are used against both men and women, they appear to be applied more harshly to women, especially when they have children; for example:

> Even my family have took it harder, the fact that I'm on drugs, than my two brothers. They've just been left to it, to get on with it. But they're more disgusted over me; being a woman and having children. (Adele, aged 26)

Family members used various strategies in attempts to monitor women's alcohol consumption. One woman explained:

> He [son] can tell as soon as he walks through the door whether I've had a drink or not, he knows straight away. But having said that when I've not drunk in weeks and weeks he's walked up to me and said, 'Have you had

a drink?' 'No I blooming well haven't; here smell my breath', you know. I got really mad. (Marjorie, aged 43)

On occasion such concerned inquiries would have the opposite effect to that intended. Angry at what she felt was an intrusion Marjorie, for example, would have a drink 'just for the hell of it'. Similarly Rachel, another problem drinker, felt that her mother was constantly checking on her, to ensure that she was not drinking; a situation which she found oppressive.

> Well every day she [mother] rings up, 'How are you?' I'm not going to tell her if I'm not all right (laughs). She is smothering me; it's too much at times. I just want a bit of space really, just a little bit of space, peace and quiet. (Rachel, aged 41)

Family controls on behaviour were not always unwelcome to women, however. One woman, for example, enlisted the help of her brother, a non-user, in her attempts to avoid drug taking. Monitoring of drinkers' and drug users' lives may be counterproductive, however, in limiting the possibilities for change in behaviour (Shephard, 1990).

Keeping Their Proper Place: Private Controls

Women who fail to 'keep their proper place' by drinking and using drugs may find their male partners leave little to chance; exerting private controls in what has been described as 'the most controversial and conflict-loaded area' (Holmila, 1991, p569). Male strategies for controlling women's behaviour documented in this study included surveillance of physical movements, controlling the supply of substances, monitoring consumption, controlling access to children, and in the more extreme cases, physical violence.

Women's activities were often personally supervised by their partners, in an occasionally breathtaking display of control. Lucy, a heavy drinker and occasional drug user, for example, described how her partner was 'very possessive, wouldn't let me go anywhere and all that.' Similarly for Adele, a heroin user, 'He'd [partner] make sure I stayed with him so I hadn't got the chance [to use drugs]'. Her subsequent partner, however, took direct control over her supply of drugs, allowing her a ration each day. The consequences of this arrangement were that her influence on family decisions was practically non existent; as a drug using woman Adele felt disqualified from holding a valued opinion.

> If he [partner] didn't like something - I didn't have an opinion on anything, on the kids, the house, or whatever he done. I was the drug taker, how dare I question anything he'd got to say? It was, 'Shut up and get on with it, or you won't be getting your money to get all your stuff [heroin] for the week'. He used to do that a lot. (Adele, aged 26)

In order to avoid such reactions women who drank alone at home often attempted to conceal their drinking; hiding from partners what they themselves felt was unacceptable behaviour. For example:

> I was using it to try and get the buzz and he didn't know, so I wasn't drinking that much. But then he started getting suspicious. He didn't say anything at first, and then he found a bottle under the bed and he said, 'You've been drinking again haven't you?', and I said, 'Yeah', and then it seemed to increase then. But I didn't binge drink and it was more a steady thing than binge drinking. I'm trying to think back to what it was like at the beginning. I wouldn't drink every day but when I did drink it was more than I should. I wasn't drunk, I always made the tea. My husband knew I'd been drinking when he came home from work. (Brenda, aged 49)

Strategies by male partners to control women's consumption of alcohol could include enlisting friends as accomplices in surveillance, as Mary explained:

> Well when I was drinking he used to try tricks like ringing a friend to come and share what I'd got, which was very annoying when I'd just stocked up nicely for myself. If he was going out to work and found my stash, he'd ring one of my friends to come and share it with me, so that I wasn't drinking alone. (Mary, aged 39)

Although Mary's partner's response could be perceived as helpful and stemming from concern on his part, he also drank heavily, and on occasion demanded that she drink with him. Whether or not her drinking was a desirable activity was, therefore, largely dependent on his needs at the time.

Where strategies to monitor their female partners activities by co-operative means failed, control of everyday activities by men could be reinforced by more overt methods, for example the implicit threat or use of violence. If non-coercive means of control were ineffective, then coercion became a potential option, and for some women in this study a terrible reality. The costs of not keeping their 'proper place' could be verbal, emotional, or physical abuse from their partners; abuse justified by their failure to behave 'properly' as women. Violence as a means of control over women by men can be seen as historically and culturally legitimised (cf. Dobash and Dobash, 1979). For example:

> Husbands who batter wives typically feel that they are exercising a right, maintaining good order in the family and punishing their wives' delinquency - especially wives' failure to keep their proper place (e.g. not doing domestic work to the husband's satisfaction, or answering back). (Connell, 1995, p213)

Anne's husband, for example, viciously attacked her when she went out drinking alone, making her fearful for the well-being of her unborn child. If she went drinking in his company, however, he was quite content and felt no necessity to exert control (cf. Thom, 1986). As Holmila (1991) points out, 'Lack of control may reflect the partner's satisfaction with the situation: if she shares the drinking with him, he has nothing to complain about' (p558). There was evidence in my study of male partners' ambivalent attitudes towards drinking, most frequently when it was a shared social activity. For example:

> Now if I have a drink he'll sort of look, it depends what mood he's in and he'll look at me and say, 'You shouldn't you know, you're getting back to what you used to be', and I'm thinking, 'He's right'. Then other days I can not have a drink 'till, like if he's doing some DIY, and I'll say, 'I'm going to have a drink', and he'll say, 'Thank God for that, I was dying for a can of lager'. (Kayleigh, aged 37)

> He [husband] liked me to have a drink with him; if I was on the wagon he often seemed to be trying to make me drink. He would get annoyed because I didn't want to have a drink with him. (Mary, aged 39)

Drug habits which were shared with partners were common amongst women in my study, and typically seen as a 'normal' part of such relationships. This was a source of concern for Emily's partner, however, who would try in a somewhat ineffectual way, to monitor their joint activities, as she explained:

> Looking back in retrospect he made us laugh, because I'd have it [amphetamine] and he'd be, 'Be careful, are you all right?', and if I managed to have a bad hit and bruised myself or something, he'd be, 'Oh, God, what's happened?' So he was concerned, but in a crazy kind of way like. And like, we'd have a couple of bags, and he'd say, 'Oh no, don't have any more, you've had enough'. It was like a load of crap

> really, because I was getting twice as much as him. But he was off his head, and thinking he was monitoring us, and things were going to be safer like. (Emily, aged 28)

The effectiveness of attempts to exert control were therefore undermined by partners sharing drugs, and the generally chaotic nature of their lifestyle. It is interesting, though, that Emily's male partner apparently felt he should take the responsibility for controlling their drug use, even if it was 'in a crazy kind of way'. This monitoring could be viewed as a type of benevolent control.

Control of behaviour by partners was not always unwelcome, however. One young woman described how she would ask her partner to prevent her obtaining drugs:

> I'd say to him [partner], 'Please, the next time I want to go out and score [heroin], tell me no'. (Emma, aged 24)

Emma's attempts were largely unsuccessful, however, as her partner was also a drug user and therefore reluctant to co-operate with her wishes.

Separation or divorce from male partners did not necessarily mean an end to controlling behaviour. Where a couple had dependent children, withholding contact with them could be used as a device to punish the mother. Jenny, a problem drinker, for example, described her husband's attempts to prevent her from seeing her children, and effectively exclude her from their lives. He was successful in this, despite the fact that he also drank heavily and was occasionally violent. As she explained:

> He [husband] got the house, he got the kids, he got the furniture, he got the cat and the dog.
>
> *How did he manage all that because usually...?*
>
> I got nothing. He put his case down to, I had a drink problem and I was homeless; I had nowhere to stay. (Jenny, aged 49)

Custody of children could also be used as a strategy for remaining in contact with their mother, even in cases where the male partner had previously been violent towards her. Social services staff could be enlisted as allies of the father; separation from the children being justified by the woman's drinking or drug use. For example:

He [partner] was phoning social services saying, 'She's drunk, she's not a fit mother', and all those sort of things, making things worse.

I could see the children. He looked after them during the day and the foster parents looked after them at night. So if I wanted to see them I had to see him. So it was basically putting up with him, his drunkenness. (Lucy, aged 33)

As Lucy's partner had been violent towards her on numerous occasions, access arrangements which meant that if she wanted to see her children she also had to risk seeing her abusive partner were unacceptable to her.

I am not suggesting that in these cases there were no problems with the mothers' ability to care for their children, but where there was doubt about the fathers' capacity to provide care, similar behaviour on their part did not appear to result in enforced separation.

The concept of a 'continuum of control' employed by men (Green *et al.*, 1987), ranging from control by consent to control by physical violence, is useful in understanding the type of control strategies used by male partners of women study participants. Where informal sanctions failed to achieve the desired result threatened or actual violence could be employed. However, women themselves were often active negotiators in relationships; accepting a degree of control from male partners in exchange for certain advantages, as I shall go on to explain.

Striking a 'Bargain'

Social control by consent may not be experienced by those women involved as control (Hutter and Williams, 1981) if it carries sufficient personal and social benefits. Rosenbaum, for example, explained the type of arrangement often experienced by women heroin users and their male partners.

Because women see themselves as providees, they often feel they can relax in the day-to-day struggles of the financial maintenance of a heroin habit, particularly if they are living with another addict. He is the man, the breadwinner, provider; hence the woman will often 'sit back' and let the man provide the drugs for her under the auspices of being a homemaker or housewife. (Rosenbaum, 1981, p867)

A number of women in the study, particularly amongst the younger group of drug users and chaotic drinkers, were aware that they had struck a type of 'bargain' (albeit unspoken) with their male partners; protection (of a sort) and a degree of economic stability, in return for acceptance of certain constraints and conditions; a bargain which often included being on the receiving end of violence. This type of bargaining between men and women was identified by Kandiyoti (1988) as one in which 'women strategize within a set of concrete constraints that reveal and define the blueprint of what I will term the *patriarchal bargain*[1] of any given society' (p275). The advantages of such strategies for women in my study, and the type of security on offer often outweighed the disadvantages of abusive relationships. For example:

> I told you that I'd stopped drinking for the first time in my life since I was eleven. I gave birth to the baby and I was the happiest person apart from I still wasn't happy in the relationship, but I thought, 'Well it's not that bad, it could be worse, he's got a job, he's hard working, he's bringing money in. I've got nice things around me; he loves kids, the oldest one'. (Lucy, aged 33)

For Lucy, however, as her partner's violence escalated and the reality of her situation became more apparent, this somewhat tentative compromise turned sour. The perceived costs attached to economic dependency on her partner began to outweigh the benefits, with the result that the relationship eventually broke down.

The primary motivation for some women in accepting controlling behaviour on the part of their male partners was obtaining a ready supply of drugs, something which they felt would otherwise be difficult for them. For example:

> I always used to be the sort of person who would never, if somebody used to say to me, 'You're not going out tonight with your friends', I'd just say, 'That's what you think', and go anyway. I wouldn't ever let anybody stand in my way, I wouldn't let anybody treat me like an idiot. But I found myself, if he'd say like, if I'd done something or he'd say, 'I've seen you in town today, why didn't you say you were in town, why did you say you were somewhere else?', something stupid like that. I knew I had to get my gear [heroin] off him that day, I found myself where normally I would have just said, 'Sack it' and walked out, I wouldn't have been able to do that. I found myself really lowering myself. He'd talk down to me or anything and I'd have to take it, I knew I'd have to take it, I'd be thinking, 'What am I going to do tomorrow if I walk out now?' (Lauren, aged 23)

Lauren's willingness to 'lower' herself reflected both her dependency on the drug and her partner's ability to provide it. The balance of power within the relationship was therefore firmly skewed in favour of her male partner. Joanne, another heroin user, was similarly reliant on her partner's ability to supply her drugs, as she explained:

> Well, when I started going out with that lad, he'd start fetching methadone up for me everyday; but we used to fall out a lot, but he used to like batter me and that, and he were very possessive. So I just thought well if we had an argument and that, I'd be stuck without my methadone. I relied on him and that you see.

> He had that much of a hang on me, with the gear [heroin]. I weren't a shoplifter, I weren't that good at sticking up for myself, and he basically knew where he had me. He was one of those, he'd always hunt me down, whichever house I were in he'd be stood outside, or waiting outside work for me. It was like I could never get away from him, you know. (Joanne, age 28)

Despite Joanne's dislike of her partner's behaviour, which included extreme jealousy and violence, she was willing to tolerate it, to keep her side of the 'bargain'. As a result she found, 'I weren't living a life at all'. Control could in this case be seen as by mutual consent, with the option of coercion reserved as a privilege of the male partner (Green *et al.*, 1987).

Similarly Adele was also prepared to relinquish control over her drug taking, in return for financial security for herself and her daughter and a ready supply of heroin. She complied with her partner's insistence that he monitor her supply of drugs, 'I'd get it all at the beginning of the week, give it him. Before he'd go to work he'd give me one every day'. Adele's acceptance of the status quo in the relationship eventually became strained, however, as she began to feel 'used and abused'. She explained:

> I thought that I was in control, I was getting my kids whatever they needed, and I was getting all the money I needed. I was living with a man I didn't love, and I actually hated being there. But I was willing to put up with it because there was a roof over our heads, a beautiful home. I just got sick of it. I didn't look at it at first as standing on my own two feet, I was more angry. I thought, 'This man's got me under his thumb'. When I really faced up to it, if he said, 'Jump', it was, 'How high?' (Adele, aged 26)

Adele finally rejected the nature of the 'bargain' with her partner as exacting too high a price in terms of self esteem, as the illusion of being in control on her part gradually faded.

Some women, however, found it difficult to distinguish between their feelings for their partner and their cravings for the drug. Chelsea's relationship, for example, was a violent one; her boyfriend would 'batter' her. Despite this the relationship lasted for six years, with drug using as its central focus. I asked her why, if the partnership was destructive, she stayed with him for so long? She replied:

> At one time I thought I'd never get over him because I did love him. I thought because of the drugs as well it were addiction to him, I had an addiction to being with him. Because I thought, 'He's got gear so I can use his gear'. (Chelsea, aged 21)

Chelsea did, however, finally leave her partner to enter drug treatment. Awareness of their situations was insufficient however, in the absence of viable alternatives, to allow some women, particularly amongst the older group, to make the break with abusive partners. As Brittan and Maynard (1984) point out, 'The fact that one knows one is in a prison does not mean that the walls will come tumbling down' (p88).

There was also evidence in the study of 'bargains' being struck between women and their male drug dealers. In these type of situations, although the dealers were usually firmly in control of transactions, there was one notable exception. Emma, a heroin user, for example, explained her arrangement:

> I suppose women can manipulate men in a way too. There was one dealer would give me drugs for free - I never gave him anything in return. But I had it put to me, why would he give me drugs, you know? I suppose it was because I was a woman. (Emma, aged 24)

Emma was unusual, however, in that her side of the bargain with the dealer involved no (immediate) financial or sexual costs to herself. In Sargent's (1992) study, for example, dealers provided free drugs for women in the expectation of receiving sexual favours in return; in what she describes as 'sexual bartering'. Veronica, an amphetamine user interviewed in this study, exchanged sex for drugs on occasion, in addition to helping bag drugs for her dealer. She was also in debt to him, and therefore felt under an obligation. Amongst the younger women in this study (although not exclusively) however, there were signs of resistance to informal controls exerted by male partners and dealers.

Resistance Tactics

Women did not always comply with what they saw as stereotypical male expectations of them. Some younger women, for example, expressed their dissent by taking on the role of 'honorary male' in the drinking or drug using community, holding their own in drinking, drug taking, dealing or stealing, and actively rejecting the secondary role assigned to them. This can provide them with a status which is otherwise lacking in their lives. As Emily explained, for example:

> I think that's one of the reasons I got into such a state, proving myself. 'Cause I was this women in this male environment and the lads'd come in and say, 'I've got some drugs here.' And he'd [partner] say, 'Why are you hiding from Emily?' 'Cause I'd be the first to say, 'Come on, gi' us a dig' [laughs]. Absolutely gob smacked, like, eh. And it was like, one thing which used to annoy me more than anything was like...women going to score was like very...it was always the men who do it, a very male thing it is. It was like, the woman stays at home and waits for the husband to return with the drugs [laughs]. If there's any left. Aye, stuff that [laughs]. So I very quickly made my mark. I said, 'If you'll sell to him, you'll sell to me.' And people would come with gear and immediately start talking to W. [husband]. And W. would say, 'It's got nothing to do with me'. And it was, 'If you want to deal, you deal with me'. 'Cause we used to sell a lot of pot [marijuana] as well. And it was me that ran the business, 'cause he's hopeless with money. He can't add two and two, like really [laughs]. He just couldn't keep on top of it, so I dealt with the guy we got the dope off and then I'd cut it up and deal it out to people like. And it very quickly got known, you deal with me like. But then I got to be known as the honorary male. I always got a kick out of scoring, particularly if I was going to meet someone new. (Emily, aged 28)

Such women talked about not being 'typical girls' or being 'tomboys', of being more at home in the company of men. The advantages of taking on this role were felt as increased powerfulness, as one woman's experience illustrates:

> I've always been a tomboy. I've always hung round with the lads. I've always wanted to be one of the lads. I can drink just as much; it's a macho type of thing. As a female I had this power. I was so powerful with the drink, I could do anything. I wasn't frightened of anything; I'd fight anybody that came the wrong way. (Lucy, aged 33)

Lucy also felt that she was 'sort of respected' by her male drinking companions, as a woman who could hold her drink. Taking on a masculine role as a form of self defence mechanism could be liberating therefore, at least in part (cf. Rosaldo and Lamphere, 1974), but the role is difficult to maintain in 'straight' society. Women becoming actively involved with the drug using and drinking fraternity could find it difficult to sustain therefore. As Sargent explains, with regard to drug dealing, for example:

> The intrusion of a woman in what is regarded as a male preserve is resented, and she must be strong and determined, and prepared to use and endure violence. (Sargent, 1992, p115)

Lucy, for example, found it necessary to take a male 'protector' within her predominantly male drinking circle, a tactic which later backfired as he began to abuse her physically. There were other problems for women who became drug dealers, as Bev explained:

> With them [women] selling drugs, and physical threats - they [male customers] don't have to pay and she can do nothing about it, stuff like that. You've generally got partners, or very close contacts, who'll look after [supply] the women, especially if it's heroin. (Bev, aged 35)

Although some women challenge the gendered status quo, therefore, by claiming male authority in the drug using or drinking world this strategy tends not to survive any determined male resistance. As Taylor (1993) notes, concerning female heroin users in her study, an awareness of the inequalities in their situation does not necessarily allow them to effect change. Attempts to do so may be countered by ingrained sexist attitudes and behaviour on the part of male partners and dealers. Women are still considered as 'commodities and fringe people', as 'peripheral participants' in the drug scene (Sargent, 1992, p118). As Kandiyoti (1988) argues, the nature of the patriarchal bargain influences both women's potential to resist oppression and the ways open for them to do so. The opportunity to create an alternative female public world, through establishing social ties, is one which is difficult to establish for many women; their circumstances preclude it. The first opportunity for many women substance misusers to do so is when they enter rehabilitation, and encounter women with similar histories and problems. Even there, however, in mixed-sex facilities, their minority status militates against developing effective challenges to male authority in their personal lives, and finding alternative strategies for survival.

Resistance on the part of women to fulfilling their usual roles, particularly in the drugs world, can be perceived as a threat to the established pecking order (Hutter and Williams, 1981). Such bids for independence are likely, therefore, to attract opposition from those (male partners and dealers) with vested interests in maintaining the normative gendered balance of power.

Conclusions

In this chapter I have described the different ways in which women drinkers and drug users' lives are controlled, either by themselves, or by others. The role of male partners in controlling women's behaviour is emphasised; however I also explain how women negotiate with male partners to strike 'bargains', and examine the tactics women use to resist private controls.

The need to be in control of one's actions at all times is historically and culturally specific to women. However, as Ettorre and Riska (1995) point out, 'Women seldom have control over their lives to the extent that men do' (p116). A common strategy amongst women in my study, particularly, but not exclusively women with children, was using alcohol and drugs as a strategy for remaining in control of everyday events. Within the domestic sphere such control was often aimed at achieving a semblance of 'normality', in doing what women usually do. The danger of losing control associated with alcohol and drugs was for some women a factor in their decisions to stop using. They were then faced with the problems of 'getting straight'; that is in controlling or ceasing drinking or drug use.

In public, despite some relaxation in attitudes towards women's social drinking, the double standard with regard to women who drink or use drugs still flourishes, with condemnation particularly directed towards women as mothers, or potential mothers. Similarly in private, within families, a common response was to try to monitor and control the user's behaviour. Although the motivation behind such controls was usually concern such strategies were largely ineffective, and could be resented by the recipient. Such personal monitoring can be seen as a type of support, but one which is, in the main, dysfunctional in its effects.

Male partners played a primary role in controlling women's behaviour. In addition to surveillance of their movements, controlling access to drugs and monitoring consumption, controls could include overtly coercive measures, such as physical or sexual violence. Women's tolerance of their partners' controlling and often abusive behaviour was a notable element of their stories. The power to impose controls in relationships could be seen as perpetuated by mutual consent, as part of the 'bargain' negotiated by women with partners. However, equally striking was the willingness of some women (particularly amongst the younger group) to challenge male power and authority on their own territory. The ability of women to mount such challenges from a position of strength and resist controlling measures, however, was limited by social and cultural factors which reinforce the power of men, in public and private. Economic dependency, for example, played a major part in women's willingness to continue relationships with male partners, exacerbated by the need to obtain alcohol or drugs in sufficient quantities, and complicated by emotional dependency. Unless they had some means of obtaining an independent income, or sufficient external support to enable them to leave abusive partners, their alternatives were few.

Rosaldo and Lamphere (1974) identify two main strategies available to women in challenging male authority; either taking on a male role, or 'establishing a sense of rank, order, and value in a world in which women prevail' (p36). Opportunities to forge links with other women were often limited, however, both by their relative lack of status within the drugs world, and by their social isolation. Because women live in 'a world permeated by the male point of view, by self-esteem and power filtered through relationships with men' (Stanko, 1985, p79) alternatives to dependency on a male partner may seem elusive, less desirable, or less legitimate. The success of women's attempts to 'rewrite the script' as individuals was constrained, therefore by the choices open to women and the extent to which they were accepted or resisted by others.

In this respect relationships between women substance users and their male partners could be seen to be part of the 'normal' continuum of male/female relationships, albeit existing at the more volatile extreme. Changes in the balance of power in relationships were often resisted, by overt or covert means, by men. The 'maximum benefit' in the negotiations between women and their male partners was in the main experienced by the men, whose ability to manipulate and control women, often by violent means, was reinforced by the added dimension of drug use.

Note

[1] Kandiyoti (1988) describes the 'patriarchal bargain' as '...the existence of set rules and scripts regulating gender relations, to which both genders accommodate and acquiesce, yet which may nontheless be contested, redefined and renegotiated.' She also notes that, '...women as a rule bargain from a weaker position' (p286).

4 Significant Others: Influences on Problem Recognition and Help-Seeking

Introduction

Women face different barriers to men in recognising a problem as drug or drink-related, and in seeking help from treatment services. Problems in their lives may be attributed to other factors, if they are acknowledged at all, while fear of social disapproval may result in the concealment of drinking and drug use (Blume, 1990; Plant, 1997). It is argued that part of the motivation for change involves the initial recognition of a problem, interpretations of it, and judgements about its severity (Murphy and Bentall, 1992). However, such decisions are not made in a social vacuum; other people, particularly male partners, family members and friends, play an important role in influencing women's decisions to admit or conceal problems, and in encouraging or inhibiting constructive action. There are physical, emotional and social consequences of drinking and drug use specific to women (cf. Davison and Marshall, 1996), which may be exacerbated by delays in seeking specialist help; at worst resulting in a slide into physical or psychological crisis. An understanding of the influences of significant others on women, and the ways in which these are affected by gender, is therefore crucial.

In the first section of this chapter, therefore, I examine the extent to which women in my study acknowledged drug taking and drinking as problematic, whether they concealed their behaviour from others, and if so, the underlying reasons for this. I also examine family responses to female drinkers and drug users, and the extent to which such responses are influenced by gender. A refusal to accept substance use as a problem on the part of a woman user may be reinforced by significant others in her immediate social network; for example:

> A conspiracy of silence within the family network often protects the female alcoholic. If a woman has retreated into the home to drink, her

55

non-visibility has fewer social consequences than for most men. The family may collude, picking up various dimensions of her normal role, refusing to share or acknowledge the problem. (Smith, 1992b, p6)

However, family criticism or support has also been identified by researchers as a powerful incentive for a woman to seek help (Beckman and Amaro, 1984; Smith, 1992b).

The influence of friends and social networks on women struggling with drug or alcohol problems is also examined in this chapter. Types of friendship networks experienced by female substance misusers are highlighted by researchers, suggesting, for example, that women who drink heavily may mix socially with others of similar tendencies. Some social networks, therefore, may inhibit problem recognition and hinder help-seeking behaviour, as Thom argues:

> ...certain types of lay networks restrict the use of specialist services by providing both an alternative form of support and, often, an alternative set of beliefs about the problem and about the use of professional help. (Thom, 1984, p380)

Family relationships and friendship networks can either have an a incentive effect, therefore, in persuading a woman to seek treatment, or precisely the opposite effect, by erecting informal barriers to professional help.

Male partners who use drugs or drink heavily have been identified as significant actors in influencing women's help-seeking behaviour, often negatively (Thom, 1986, 1987; Smith, 1992b; Gossop, Griffiths and Strang, 1994). If a woman has a drinking problem, for example, living with a partner who also drinks heavily may be a strong disincentive to seeking help, particularly if he is unwilling to change his behaviour. In some cases husbands or partners may deliberately undermine a woman's efforts to stop drinking. For example, a participant in Thom's (1986) study commented that, 'When we got home [from hospital] he put a bottle right in front of me poured it out and put it into my hands' (p782). Similarly two-thirds of those questioned in a study of women using alcohol treatment facilities described their husbands as unsympathetic with their efforts to cut down on their drinking (Smith, 1992a).

In the case of illegal drugs such as heroin or cocaine, male partners may be active in procuring drugs, dealing to others and sharing supplies with their partners (Sargent, 1992; Taylor, 1993). Taking drugs can become the basis of a whole way of life in a relationship, which may be threatened by a woman attempting to change her behaviour. Taylor (1993) for example, suggests that the effects of a partner continuing to use drugs may undermine a woman's efforts to seek help. Female heroin users, for example, who live with male drug users, may therefore be both deprived of the protective effects of social support, and exposed to additional risks (for example, of relapse after treatment) (Gossop *et al.,* 1994).

In this chapter, therefore, I explore the ways in which male partners inhibited help-seeking on the part of women study participants, and the strategies they employed in resisting change. Drawing on theories developed primarily in relation to domestic violence, I also consider how contemporary ideas concerning privacy in family life may reinforce women's difficulties in obtaining outside help for drinking and drug problems.

'The Best Actresses in the World': Problem Denial

> I think when you're in denial, if you've got a problem, be it drink, drugs, or whatever, if you're in denial of that then you can't really do anything about it. It's only when you acknowledge it as a problem you can look at the problem; if you're in denial about it then you haven't really got a problem. (Veronica, aged 32)

A striking feature of the findings of my study was the number of women who concealed their alcohol or drug use from others, or denied outright the existence of a problem. Twelve women (52% of the sample) in my study described doing this; these were evenly divided between those whose primary drug of choice was alcohol, and those who used heroin or amphetamines, or a combination of alcohol and illegal drugs. Their reasons for concealment or denial were largely concerned with issues around close relationships, involving partners, family members and friends. The anticipated negative reaction of others was a strong influence on these women, as was embarrassment, as Audrey, a problem drinker's experience illustrates.

> I'm embarrassed, I feel like a complete failure. I think people will think less of me, so I've decided not to tell people. (Audrey, aged 25)

Similarly:

> I haven't got to the point where I can talk openly about it; only very few people know that I have got a problem. I would be embarrassed for people to know. (Mary, aged 39)

By remaining silent about their problems, even within close family circles, women could avoid adverse reactions from others, at least in the short-term.

Many female respondents expressed fears that they were failing other members of their families, frequently a source of regret for them. As Edna explained, after admitting to her brothers that she had a drinking problem, 'I felt ashamed of it; I felt I'd let them down'. Feelings of fear were often associated with the anticipation of losing other people's respect, of being judged and found wanting. Denials were often maintained even in the face of direct accusations; for example when Lauren's mother challenged her about her heroin use she replied vehemently, 'It's not me, it's you. I'm not doing anything wrong. I'm not up to anything'. Over a period of time such behaviour could become habitual, as Emily, an amphetamine user, explained: 'That's the thing with being a drugtaker, you see, you become one of the best actresses in the world'.

Implicit in these accounts of denial is a degree of self protection; for example Emma, a young heroin user, said, 'I was lying, I suppose, to save myself, and anybody knowing how bad I was'. However, such decisions concerning concealment are not gender neutral; they reflect the underlying knowledge that society is likely to respond more harshly towards women, than towards men in similar circumstances. The fear of rejection experienced by women drug users also reflects a desire to protect others, particularly those who are seen to be vulnerable. This included, for example, elderly people or young children; those to whom women would normally offer care. Two examples illustrate this point:

> I tried to keep it from my father for quite a while because he's 84 and quite frail. But it was obvious I was drinking and he knew that. So he was quite upset. (Brenda, aged 49)

> I'd hide it [from the children] in cherryade; half would be vodka and the rest would be cherryade. I'd be looking like I was supping cherryade. (Rachel, aged 41)

Both women with alcohol and drug problems described attempting to protect people close to them in this way, with varying degrees of success. It was not only elderly people and children who were seen as vulnerable, however; parents and partners were also shielded from the worst aspects of problems. Because women are, in general, the caretakers of society, both informally, in the home, and formally in jobs which contain an element of caring for others (Bryson, 1992), it goes against the grain in a fundamental way to be seen as failing in their appointed roles. Women are regarded as morally responsible for the maintenance of the family unit, providing personal services for other members of their families; therefore subsuming their own needs in favour of those of others is simply an extension of what they are accustomed to doing (Pahl, 1985). By continuing to fulfil their 'normal' domestic roles for as long as possible, a number of women found they could avert both suspicion and criticism from others. As Adele explained:

> I got away with it [heroin use] for a long time. Maybe because I had a good home, and I had the money from my partner working. I was always clean and cooked for the kids, so my family took a while [to find out]...(Adele, aged 26)

Because women anticipate more negative reactions to their drug use and drinking than men their reluctance to discuss their problems, even with intimates, is understandable. A number of respondents found that other people were also willing to attribute their problems to other, more socially acceptable causes, such as depression or anxiety (Koffinke, 1991). For example:

> ... everybody knows I like a drink, so does my brother, but they honestly thought it was because of the situation in - two relationships breaking down, constantly financially in difficulties, constantly struggling with this maintenance...(Sue, aged 47)

This type of diversionary tactic could be acceptable to women users, as it was to Sue, because it reinforced their belief that they did not really have problems with alcohol or drugs. They were content to collude with other people to disguise the true nature of their problems (Thom, 1984; Massella, 1991).

← "behavioural problem not alcohol"
 - homeless situation, who they were with etc......

Gendered Expectations (or 'I want my daughter back')

The influences of other family members on women's help-seeking are not clear cut. In my study, for example, they were both positive and negative; furthermore, individual family members reacted differently to substance misusers and their responses often changed over time. However, there are certain responses which can be seen to be gender-specific, relating to expectations of behaviour, and clearly illustrating the gendered nature of problem recognition.

Drug use in both men and women frequently disrupts family life and destroys expectations for the future (Donoghoe *et al.*, 1987; Dorn, Ribbens and South, 1987); however, in female offspring it contravenes parental expectations in a fundamental way. Parents of the younger group of drug users in this study, for example, were especially traumatised by their daughters' drug use, even in families where male siblings were also known drug users. In some cases this affected their ability to recognise the existence of a problem. Chelsea, for example, a long-term heroin user, explained that her father did not take her problem seriously and that, 'He probably didn't want to believe it'. Lauren also described her father's reaction to discovering her drug habit:

> ...my dad used to keep telling me, 'I want my daughter back, I want the
> girl that I used to have'. (Lauren, aged 23)

The shock experienced by Lauren's parents at her revelations was intense;
they did not expect to encounter such problems in their family, particularly
with their daughter. When, on one occasion, the police contacted Lauren's
mother and told her that her daughter was in custody for theft, she replied:

> 'Oh no, don't you mean my son?' They [police] went, 'No, we mean your
> daughter'. My mum said, 'You must have got it wrong, you must mean
> my son'. (Lauren, aged 23)

Similarly, Adele, another heroin user, found that her family reacted more
harshly to her drug use than to that of her brothers; they were more
'disgusted' over her behaviour. A common response by family members to
the dawning recognition of a woman's alcohol or drug problem was that of
anger and attributing blame. Often the anger felt towards the user was
expressed verbally in insults or accusations. Joanne's parents, for example,
told her that she was a 'smackhead' and 'not a fit mother'. In some cases
this type of response can be seen to relate to normative expectations of
female behaviour; women should behave 'properly', responsibly, and if they
have children be good mothers. There were differences, however in the ways
in which individual family members responded to women's drinking and drug
use. Ali (aged 20,) for example, was distressed by her mother accusing her
of selfishness and of being 'not fit to be a mother'; her father, however, was
more understanding of the stresses involved in single parenthood, and more
frequently offered her sympathy and support.

Donoghoe and his colleagues (1987) suggest that women are particularly
hard hit when their children become involved in drug using, because they
invest so much of themselves in the mother-child relationship. The elements
of caring, the labour and the love, which Hillary Graham (1984) described
as characteristic of a mother's role, come under threat, when their long-term
expectations for their children are shattered by the discovery of drug use.
Following the initial shock, a period of grief may occur (Donoghoe *et al.*,
1987). In this study Emma, for example, shielded her mother from the
knowledge of her drug use because she felt it would 'break her heart', while
Lauren's mother actually attempted suicide on learning of her daughter's
drug habit.

Evidence from this study further suggests that in addition to the greater
impact on mothers, parental reactions to drug use or problem drinking may
also vary according to the gender of the child, in that differential
expectations of female children may intensify feelings of shock, stigma and
loss.

Friendships: 'Part of the Scene'

Social drinking and drug use was common, particularly amongst the younger women in the study, with the result that defining behaviour as a problem could be inhibited, as it was a shared experience. This was less so for the older, predominantly alcohol using women, who were more likely to report friends as a positive, supportive influence in their lives (although three women in this group had no close friends).

Veronica's experience with a drug using friend, for example, illustrates the social reinforcement provided by the type of relationship which was based on drug sharing.

> ...we were quite similar in lots of ways. We liked the same kind of music, depressing stuff [laughs], things like that. So we were quite similar really; she's into self mutilating as well. We wanted to die at the same time; we sat in a church yard drinking, talking about death, and taking loads of paracetamol. (Veronica, aged 32)

With other friends, however, she shared more casual drinking sessions, where the primary aim was 'having a laugh'. Other women reported similar experiences, for example:

> ...friends thought I was top laugh believe it or not, getting plastered and doing daft things. They just said I was a town girl. (Audrey, aged 25)

In this type of social environment there was little remarkable about Veronica and Audrey's behaviour. Even if close friends became concerned it was easy for problematic drinking to be explained away as just part of the social scene. As Thom points out:

> ...being involved with a group of drinking friends, would appear not only to incur a greater risk of developing a drink problem but also to provide a social context and a set of beliefs about drinking which act as a barrier to the definition of drink as a problem requiring treatment. (Thom, 1984, p381)

A similar argument could be applied to casual or 'recreational' drug use; in certain circumstances taking drugs is seen as an accepted (almost required) part of social life, and not as a 'problem (Rosenbaum, 1981; Wister and Avison, 1982).

Paradoxically, however, attempts by a woman to step outside the 'scene' and seek help for her habit could also meet with resistance. Amongst Veronica's friends, for example, the general view expressed concerning her entrance to rehabilitation was that, 'She'll last five weeks'. Not only therefore was problem recognition inhibited for this group of women, but help-seeking outside the established circle was often unwelcome, as relationships with drug using or drinking 'buddies' could be threatened by change. Emily, for example, described her friends' reactions to her entering treatment for amphetamine use.

> It's funny but the ones who take drugs are the ones who are a bit stand offish. They're perfectly fine with you when you see them...but there are the ones that don't come near. It's been with friends that don't take drugs at all or take a very small amount of drugs are the ones that are phoning, and the ones that are bothered about us. (Emily, aged 28)

By changing their behaviour these women, to varying degrees, became the 'deviants', the outsiders in their social circles. Maintaining motivation to continue treatment in the face of such influences, therefore, required great determination and strength of character (not attributes normally associated with problem drinkers and drug users). In general, however, the impact of peers on problem recognition and help-seeking was felt to a greater degree by the younger group of women in the study.

Partners: The 'Drug Bond'

For the majority of women in this study (most notably amongst the younger group) male partners emerged as negative influences on help-seeking, particularly in those cases where both partners used drugs, or drank heavily. The behavioural reinforcement experienced by women living with a partner who also uses has been identified by several previous studies of female drug users (for example, Rosenbaum, 1981; Sargent, 1992). Kantor and Straus (1989) describe this type of relationship, which can be both a source of comfort and conflict to the participants, as one based on a 'drug bond'.

Although some women are introduced to drugs by female friends the most common pattern is for men to initiate women into drug use (Hser, Anglin and Booth, 1987; Parker *et al.*, 1988; Almog, Anglin and Fisher, 1993). Joanne, for example, explained that, 'I always had my [heroin] habit supported for me' (by her male partner). Although being supplied with drugs by a male partner is common among female users, they may be expected to steal or prostitute themselves to make their financial contribution (Sargent, 1992; Taylor, 1993). Several women in my study, for example, described taking part in shop-lifting or stealing in support of their own and their partners' drug habits.

When drug taking was a shared experience it was difficult for one partner to put up a token show of resistance to the other partner using, even if they were concerned for the consequences. As one young woman explained:

With living with my boyfriend, and both of us using, it's a lot harder. Because one day you might be feeling strong, but the other person feels weak. And it only takes them to say, 'Go on', and you'll do it. There's someone else in the same mess as you, so you know how each other feels. (Emma, aged 24)

Similarly, Emily, who shared her amphetamine habit with her husband, found that although, 'He put himself through a lot of guilt for it, he didn't stop, he didn't help in any way. Because by then he had a bigger problem'.

The sharing of drugs between partners has the potential to lead to a situation spiralling out of control. A scarcity of the desired drug, however, may also cause problems. Women could suffer violent repercussions, for example, if the supply of drugs was not forthcoming.

Shared drinking sessions with male partners were also common occurrences for these women. Sue (aged 47), for example, explained that her partner 'used to drink with me, even though it was causing a lot of problems'. This type of ambivalence towards their problem drinking was experienced by five women; partners on the one hand expressing concern about the habit, while on the other tacitly encouraging it. Drinking heavily for men may be perceived as culturally 'normal', if not actually socially encouraged (Ussher, 1998); their behaviour, therefore, may not attract critical attention to the same extent as their female partners'.

Although relationships with male partners had the potential to be supportive and non-exploitative, these were comparatively rare amongst study participants. It was more usual that joint alcohol or drug use, or factors associated with a relationship (including violence), were influential in maintaining a dependency on substances, or in its escalation into chaotic use (cf. Hser *et al.*, 1987).

There were differences evident, however, in the responses of male partners of the older group (aged over 35) of primarily problem drinking women and the younger (aged 35 and under) primarily drug-using (or chaotic drinking and drug-using) women. Those women reporting the influence of partners as wholly negative were more likely to be found in the younger group; six women describing their partners as exerting predominantly negative influences on help-seeking, and four a combination of positive and negative influences. Amongst the older group of problem drinking women the situation was less clear-cut; the majority of this group experiencing their partners as either ambivalent towards them seeking help, or as having no discernible influence. Unambiguous, positive support from male partners in getting 'straight' was a scarce commodity, however, for both groups of women.

The nature of relationships in which drug using is a central feature appears to militate against male partners exerting a positive influence on help-seeking. This probably reflects the dominant role played by men in these relationships, in supplying and sharing drugs with their partners (Gossop, Griffiths and Strang, 1988, 1994; Daly, 1992; Sargent, 1992). As Daly points out:

> Drug using partners of women do not want to lose a grafting (offence committing) partner. Nor indeed do they want to lose a partner who is by default dependent on them because of their drug dependence, since the male has power as the procurer of drugs. (Daly, 1992, p18)

Joanne said of her male partner, for example, in relation to his role as supplier of drugs to her and others, 'He just loved that power'. If shared drug use was not defined as a problem by the dominant (male) partner, therefore, than help-seeking could be delayed or discouraged entirely.

When such practices and attitudes are an integral part of an intimate relationship, change on the part of the individual can be seen as threatening to the status quo, as I shall go on to explain. There were several types of negative influence exerted by women's partners, who can be seen as covertly or overtly resisting change; these included physical or emotional distancing, refusal to accept the existence of a problem, and open encouragement to drink or use drugs.

Maintaining the Status Quo

A common reaction experienced by women in the study was that of male partners distancing themselves, either physically or emotionally, from their problems. Brenda, for example, described her husband's reaction to her drinking, and the effect it had on her.

> My husband was backing off; I knew why he was backing off. I didn't blame him but it was not pleasant to see and in a way you want more, but people do back off you when you're drinking and in a way that's the last thing you want. You want people to come in and help you, and the people that you love most are the ones that you're hurting most, they're the ones that back off. (Brenda, aged 49)

Brenda's husband would physically separate himself from her to the extent of sitting in a different room when they were both present in their home. Although they were together in as much as they shared the same roof, he placed himself as far away from Brenda as possible. She was also subjected to violence, on the occasions when her husband was forced to confront her drinking problem.

Emotional distancing was typically used by men as a device to avoid confrontation or active involvement with a female partner's problems. Sue's partner, for example, was reluctant to discuss her drinking with her under any circumstances. If she persisted in trying to tell him of her problems he would simply disappear from her life without explanation, for days, weeks, or even months at a time, with the result that Sue's self esteem gradually diminished, and her alcohol consumption increased. A partner's refusal to recognise the existence of a problem also meant that action could be avoided; for example, as Rachel explained:

> He [husband] just saw me plodding round thinking, 'It's you that's putting it down your neck'. He didn't see it as a problem at all. (Rachel, aged 41)

Rachel's husband consequently did not see the need for her to have treatment for her drinking. Her period in residential alcohol rehabilitation, from his perspective, was an undesirable interruption to 'normal' family life; even if family life frequently included Rachel drinking heavily. Her husband's resentment at her help-seeking was expressed by his reluctance, after weekend visits home, to drive her back to the rehabilitation unit to continue treatment.

Non acceptance of a problem may therefore be another means of expressing anger towards the problem drinker or drug user, whilst avoiding the outbreak of open hostilities. It may also be an expression of resistance to change within a relationship; less threatening to the status quo than open discussion. Although there could be initial enthusiasm for women's changing behaviour on the part of male partners, this could diminish in the face of the reality. When women decided to seek help for their drinking or drug use, for example, and acted upon this, partners occasionally reacted negatively, or in such a way as to weaken motivation. Changes in relationships, particularly sexual relationships, could be seen as threatening; for example in cases where sexual activity had previously been associated with drinking or taking drugs.

> *What was his [partner's] reaction to you looking for help and trying to stop drinking?*
>
> ...he was all right, he thought it was a good idea, until I actually did. And when I stopped drinking I was no longer relying on him to do things for me. I could do things for myself. He couldn't sleep with me because I didn't want to, and most of the time it was forced because we'd had a

> drink. So he realised he no longer had me where he wanted me, because I was laying the law down and doing things for myself instead of being pathetic and hopeless, lying there ill whilst he's doing everything, running here and there and sorting everything out totally controlling my life. So he didn't like it and actually encouraged me to drink; he tried to get me to drink so he could sleep with me... (Lucy, aged 33)

The idea of changing behaviour was initially a welcome one for Lucy's partner, but the reality of it, because her incapacity had served a purpose, was threatening to the balance of power in the relationship. This response may be related to the desire of the male to retain 'exclusive ownership' over his female partner (Dobash and Dobash, 1998). A partner's willingness to support abstinence could be limited, to the extent where he would actually encourage a woman to drink or use drugs (cf. Thom, 1986). As Audrey explained:

> ...I asked him questions that made him feel very uncomfortable, and then obviously it wasn't a good idea that I was doing this. When I was detoxing, on the tenth day it was killing me - I was in tears. He said, 'Just go to the off license and get a bottle of wine if it's going to be like this'. So that was as much as he could put up with. (Audrey, aged 25)

Audrey's partner was initially keen for her to seek help for her drink problem. His attitude then altered, however, from one of offering support to a complete withdrawal of help; a change which Audrey felt was explained by a desire not to draw attention to his own behavioural problems. While their joint attention was focused on her drinking, his difficulties could be obscured, while if she sought help and 'recovered', they would be thrown into sharp relief.

Changes in women's behaviour were only welcome, therefore, when they were confinable within the parameters of a relationship, and did not challenge established patterns of behaviour. The ability of men to control and regulate women's behaviour, which is evident from these accounts, is maintained and reproduced by an ideology which emphasises that women should be prepared to sacrifice their own needs for the good of others, particularly their partners and children (Green *et al.*, 1987). If they fail if this endeavour they are expected to (and frequently do) feel guilty. Resistance to change by male partners can be further explained by considering concepts of privacy and boundary control, drawing on feminist theories of domestic violence.

Privacy and Boundary Control in Intimate Relationships

> All I know is that the loneliest I've been, the most isolated, is when I've
> lived with my family and within intimate relationships. (Bev, aged 35)

Family life in contemporary western society is bound up with ideas
concerning the privacy of the home and personal relationships, and freedom
from intrusion by outsiders. Within the family the effect of married or
cohabiting relationships for the participants is twofold; they provide a degree
of protection from outside interference, but also, to some extent, isolate them
from outside help (Pahl, 1985; Eaton, 1993). Notions of privacy within the
family may be reinforced by the 'deviant' behaviour of women substance
users; if their activities are not actually illegal, then they are certainly
socially undesirable. The impulse towards maintaining privacy is therefore
strengthened both by the illegal nature of the proceedings (in the case of drug
use), and the social stigma attached. Secrecy within the family unit may
serve to conceal something which is seen to be socially devalued; alcohol and
drug problems being the second most common type of taboo secret (the most
common being sexual secrets) (Brown-Smith, 1998).

Within the family the status of women is traditionally lower than that of
men, while in the case of illegal drug use the authority and status of the male
partner is often further emphasised by his role as provider of funds and
supplier of drugs. The benefits of privacy and lack of outside interference
may be less for women in general, therefore, and for women drug users and
drinkers in particular, than for men. For example, as Pahl argues:

> ...one function of this norm of privacy is to maintain particular power
> relations within the family. (Pahl, 1985, p39)

Concerns to maintain privacy, heightened by the knowledge of deviant
status, may therefore reinforce women's relative powerlessness within
relationships with husbands or male partners.

A tension exists concerning privacy within families or couple
relationships which involve substance misuse; between the state's need to
reveal and control drug use, and maintain social order - and the concern of
individuals to conceal deviant behaviour, maintain privacy, and thus avoid
potential sanctions. Public health is seen to be at risk from behaviours
defined as socially problematic (Smart, 1984); therefore the risk of drawing
attention to one's own behaviour (and moral failings) is great. Within a
relationship itself there may also be contradictory forces in operation; one
seeking to keep problems private, the other attempting to make them public.
This process has been referred to, in the context of help-seeking for domestic
violence, as 'boundary control' (Borkowski, Murch and Walker, 1983). The
desire to seek help for a situation which a woman perceives to be

problematic, may be in conflict with that of her partner's wish to maintain the boundary of the relationship as private. The power structure of a partnership, however, inevitably affects negotiations with outsiders. This may be particularly evident where relationships involve violence, for example:

> Social and physical isolation is a characteristic of many violent marriages. One way for a batterer to assert dominance and control over all aspects of a woman's life is to keep her isolated and dependent on his demands. (Dobash and Dobash, 1998, p43)

Because a great deal of domestic violence remains 'hidden' society's rules may be violated with few if any consequences being suffered by the perpetrator (Berardo, 1998). In a conflict model of interpersonal relationships 'nondisclosure is a strategy used to gain and maintain power over others' (Brown-Smith, 1998, p30).

Much of women's self esteem, social worth and reflected power is bound up with relationships with men; therefore the desire of male partners to preserve the privacy of the relationship is likely to prevail, although both partners may invest importance in maintaining the relationship's integrity.

> The knowledge that each one has about the other, coupled with their power to withhold it from, or communicate it to the outside world gives both some kind of hold over the other. (Borkowski *et al.*, 1983, p108)

Ideas concerning privacy within relationships, coupled with inequalities of status and power, may, therefore, be an impediment to external help-seeking for a woman, even if she has a great deal to gain by eliciting it; as contact with outsiders affects the boundary of a relationship, disturbs its essentially private nature, and may threaten disruption.

> It is hardly surprising that the weaker partner might feel the need to recruit allies and widen the audience, while the stronger may seek to prevent this. Thus the way in which the power balance of a partnership is managed may influence what information the partners choose to disclose to the outside world, how they do it, and when they choose to tell. (Borkowski *et al.*, 1983, pp.109-110)

Resistance to change (whether covert or overt) on the part of a male partner of a drug user or drinker can therefore be seen as an attempt both to maintain the boundary control of a relationship, and the balance of power within it. According to Dobash and Dobash (1998) a common cause of conflicts of interest within family life, with the potential of violent consequences, is the importance to men of maintaining their power and authority.

A woman's willingness to breach the boundary of a relationship may depend on several factors; the degree of loyalty and affection felt towards her partner; the extent of the self esteem provided by the relationship; and the alternative resources available to her, particularly those of an economic nature (Borkowski *et al.*, 1983). It will also depend, to a degree, on her perception of the type of support she is likely to receive from external sources.

Conclusions

In this chapter I have explored the ways in which problem recognition and help-seeking on the part of women are affected by gender, and how this manifests itself in aspects of personal relationships. This analysis, therefore, begins from existing knowledge concerning the influence of significant others on problem recognition and help-seeking, highlights the influence of male partners on women, and details the type of negotiations involved in such relationships; negotiations played out against a background in which familial privacy and gendered inequality are integral factors.

Women in this study often refused to admit to problems with alcohol or drugs. This was variously attributed to embarrassment, the fear of being judged, or to the desire to protect others from uncomfortable knowledge. In each case, however, it was the possibility or probability of adverse reactions, either within the family circle, or in the public sphere, which inhibited discussion. A study by Dahlgren and Myrhed (1977) noted that women who denied the existence of their problems often delayed seeking help for long periods of time, or sought it indirectly through private practitioners, gynaecologists, and family advisers. Although such denial is not exclusive to women substance misusers, in terms of stigma and negative responses from others they have more to lose than men in similar circumstances (Rosenbaum, 1981). In addition, women's normative roles as carers of others may deter them from distressing those seen as vulnerable - elderly parents or children, for example - with what they see as unnecessary or unwelcome information.

Confirming findings of previous studies, family and friends of female users were also, in some cases, willing to divert attention from substance misuse as a source of problems in favour of more neutral, less stigmatising, causes such as depression (cf. Harrison, 1989). Such misconceptions may be seized upon by women wishing to conceal their problems, as an effective smokescreen. In some cases this amounts to collusion between the user and significant others, which serves both to protect themselves from unwelcome knowledge, and to conceal such knowledge from the public gaze. The family may 'close ranks', to protect not only themselves but also the user from public disapproval (Raine, 1995).

Social expectations of female family members are gender specific; they are simply not expected to display certain types of deviant behaviour, which include excessive drinking and drug use. Such expectations may hinder problem recognition and help seeking, by obscuring the true nature of women's problems. However, when problems with alcohol and drugs did come to light the expression of anger directed at women in this study by other family members was common; these responses often related to their inability (or unwillingness) to behave as 'proper' women. Although previous studies have identified the differential impact on mothers of drug using children (Donoghoe *et al.*, 1987; Dorn *et al.*, 1987) I also argue that the gender of the child is significant when considering parental responses. Drug use by daughters appears to be particularly difficult for parents to understand and manage.

This evidence suggests, therefore, that the provision of support and information for families of female problem drinkers and drug users is of the utmost importance (Gay, 1989). Although many rehabilitation agencies, for example, do offer some version of family support, this is limited in scope, and may consist, at best, of one or two 'family sessions' per month. Community agencies are increasingly aware of the need for this type of support service, but voluntary groups may be limited in their capabilities in this respect. The type of intensive information and support sessions for family members or significant others developed by rehabilitation units such as Clouds House, in Wiltshire, may offer a useful model for service development.

Moving in social circles where drug and alcohol use was a commonplace occurrence could inhibit women, firstly from recognising the existence of a problem, and secondly, from seeking help from outside their immediate circle. As previous research has suggested, therefore, the protective effects of social support are weakened when relationships are predominantly based on sharing psychoactive substances. Amongst younger women in the study (aged 35 and under) this was a particular problem.

Drinking and taking drugs, for many women in the study, was a shared activity with male partners. It was rare, however, for a woman to take the dominant role in these partnerships. Heavy drinking, for example, would often be defined as a 'problem' for a woman, while that of her partner was seen as part of 'normal' male behaviour. Problem definition could be linked, therefore, to power relations within sexual relationships, with men claiming the lion's share of power and authority.

There was evidence in this study of ambivalence amongst male partners to women's drinking and drug use, and covert or overt resistance on their part to changing behaviour. Younger women were particularly susceptible to negative influences on help-seeking from their male partners. There was evidence, for example, of partners attempting to undermine a woman's attempts to get 'straight', where change on her part threatened the basis of attachments, and particularly the sexual element of relationships. I have linked this phenomenon to the concept of boundary control, and attempts by male partners to maintain the privacy of a relationship; attempts which are reinforced by both partners' desire to avoid drawing attention either to their joint activities, or to the 'deviant' behaviour of the female partner.

Recognising that a problem with substances exists, therefore, and being prepared to elicit help from external sources has particular difficulties for women; differences which relate to structural inequalities, both in private and public. Betsy Thom, in her work concerning women and alcohol services, explains the effects of what she describes as the 'anticipatory factor' on help-seeking.

> ...people anticipate in one stage what is to happen in the next. In particular, what it means to the individual to expose a drinking problem beyond the relatively private confines of family and friends out into the public arena, with all that implies for the drinkers' psychological and social identity, may well influence who is asked for help and whether contact with 'public' forms of help is delayed to crisis point. (Thom, 1984, p380)

Responses from 'public' agencies to women in situations of potential crisis therefore take on additional importance, as I go on to discuss in the next chapter.

5 Why Women Underuse Drug and Alcohol Treatment Services

Introduction

> Whenever Britain's drug use is talked about, while it should be recognised that the majority of users are male, it must also be remembered that between a quarter and a third are female. (ISDD, 1994, p29)

Women's under-representation as clients of formal alcohol and drug treatment agencies has been noted by numerous commentators in recent years. Where women do attend treatment they are usually in a minority; furthermore the type of services offered to women has been criticised as inadequate for their needs (Reed, 1985; Ettorre, 1992; DAWN, 1994).

There are certain factors which have been identified as encouraging women to present for alcohol and drug treatment; for example, recognition of a health problem associated with substance use; interference with work or domestic roles; problems with personal or social relationships; or pressure from partners or significant others to bring about change in behaviour (Smith, 1992b). Some women, of course, are coerced into treatment by legal agencies.

Set against these factors, women's willingness to enter treatment may be negatively affected in certain areas, which can outweigh pressures to seek help. Betsy Thom (1986) notes, for example, that 'social support networks, societal norms and the structure of treatment agencies promote inequities to women with alcohol related problems' (p777). However, there is currently a paucity of research on gender in connection with help-seeking and service use.

> There is...little research which examines women's own perceptions of the costs and benefits of entering treatment, or the actual costs experienced by those who do seek help. (Thom and Green, 1996, p207)

72

An early study concerning women in alcohol treatment was carried out by Beckman and Amaro in California; this identified several important factors affecting women's substance misuse, which included:

- Women's own perceptions of substance use and attitudes towards seeking help.

- Alcohol and drug services - professional attitudes to users, access to services, service orientation, and service options open to women. (adapted from Beckman and Amaro, 1984, Table 11-1)

In this chapter I consider each of these factors, and map out what is currently known about their impact on women's use of drug and alcohol services.

Women's Attitudes Towards Seeking Help

> ...if a drug makes you feel good it must be bad. (Ettorre *et al.*, 1994, p1671).

Women are conscious of the greater responsibility placed on them by society to avoid or limit the use of certain mind-altering substances, or only indulge in them in certain prescribed circumstances, according to previous studies; for example they experience more feelings of guilt about using minor tranquillisers than men. Similarly, many women feel guilty about drinking, worrying particularly about the effects on their capacity to care for children (Beckman and Amaro, 1984). Many of the participants in Gomberg's (1988) study of women in alcohol treatment, for example, expressed harsher attitudes about female drinking than a control group drawn from the general population, both reflecting and magnifying normative societal attitudes. This was particularly evident amongst the older group of women, aged in their forties, a greater number of whom thought that a mother's problem drinking has a more serious effect on growing children than a father's. In both the treatment and control group, however, younger women held more liberal attitudes concerning problem drinking in women.

Knowledge of the social stigma attached to substance use, particularly in relation to alcohol and illicit drugs, may lead some women to remain silent about their problems, or if they do seek help, to present to health professionals with less specific complaints. Thus a collusion between doctor and patient to avoid confronting the problem may arise. In this way barriers to obtaining professional help can be erected, as women self monitor their complaints to fit in with what is seen as normal and acceptable behaviour, with the result that:

> For mental health disorders that are congruent with accepted sex-role stereotypes (such as depression) women show higher rates of use of services than do men. In contrast, for problems such as alcoholism that are incongruent with idealised sex-role stereotypes, women show much lower (prevalence-corrected) utilisation rates than do men. (Beckman and Amaro, 1984, p331)

Even if women do decide to seek specialist help, they may remain unconvinced that drinking or drug use is their main source of difficulty (Thom, 1986). Social embarrassment concerning the nature of their problems can also be a strong disincentive to admit them publicly, as being defined and labelled as having substance use problems, because it flies in the face of gender specific expectations of behaviour, may carry with it greater negative consequences for women. Women's own perceptions and attitudes towards substance use, unsurprisingly, reflect those of the general society, although there is some evidence of a gradual liberalisation of attitudes amongst the young (Gomberg, 1988, 1993).

Women's greater awareness of health-related matters and general willingness to seek medical help may, in general, act as a trigger for help-seeking behaviour; however this may be offset by expectations of disapproval and possible censure from helping professionals. I therefore go on to discuss evidence concerning the ways in which professional responses to female substance misusers affect their access to drug and alcohol treatment.

Drug and Alcohol Treatment Services

Professional Attitudes and Women's Access to Treatment

Although women consult medical professionals more frequently than men, there is reluctance on the part of GPs and other health professionals to recognise, name and confront their problems with chemical substances (Thom and Tellez, 1986; Blume, 1990; Collins, 1993). Coupled with women's own unwillingness to present with such problems this may result in their either not being dealt with, or 'sanitised' under an alternative diagnosis of depression or anxiety. In some cases the decisions of physicians appear to be guided by stereotypes of female behaviour. Women who drink may be viewed as 'doubly deviant'; they do not fit the standards of acceptable female behaviour, neither do they conform to male patterns of alcohol use (Reed, 1987). Because they fall outside the 'norm' therefore they may attract negative, or avoiding responses from health professionals. For example, women with alcohol problems may be considered as being more difficult to treat than men who drink similarly, or the presence of alcohol as part of the presenting problem may simply not be considered (Blume, 1990). Avoidance of confrontation, embarrassment and wariness of labelling a woman as 'alcoholic' are factors identified as hindering honest exchanges between doctor and patient (Thom and Tellez, 1986). Research suggests that 'the diagnosis of drinking problems, particularly in the early stages, poses intellectual and emotional problems for general practitioners' (Smith, 1992b, p6). Furthermore, working with patients with alcohol or drug problems is not viewed by some helping professionals as a desirable part of their role, and may be avoided (Thom, 1986). The consequences of non-intervention for the user can be serious, as the following comment suggests:

> The involvement of GPs can be crucial for the drugtaker. If someone with a drug problem goes to a GP for help and does not get it, he or she can be expected to develop other more serious problems of a legal, social, medical, psychological or psychiatric kind and as a consequence the overall drug problem will worsen and become more entrenched. (Waller, 1993, p11)

There is also a tendency in dealing with substance misuse problems to medicalise or concentrate on the psychological defects of the user. Such approaches may result in treatment of the user as a 'patient', with little or no attention paid to precipitating social factors (Sargent, 1992). It is argued, for example, that health professionals readily make a psychiatric diagnosis when dealing with women, as they see them as particularly susceptible to developing emotional problems. The willingness to diagnose and prescribe particular remedies to women therefore reflects certain views of them as sensitive, overly emotional, and potentially mentally unstable (Perry, 1979).

The advantage for the professional worker of such medicalisation of women's problems is in clarification of the issues in terms of treatment and 'cure', but this may have dysfunctional aspects for the women involved. Take, for example, the case of a woman living with an abusive partner. She may complete 'treatment' only to be discharged into precisely the same situation which precipitated her problems. Treating an individual as a 'problem to be solved' patently fails to address social aspects of substance use.

In Ettorre and her colleagues' (1994) study of minor tranquilliser use, for example, it was discovered that, when women expressed a desire to cease using such drugs, they were offered support from their physicians to a much lesser extent than men. Twice as many male users as women were helped by their GPs in reducing or withdrawing from tranquilliser use. As physicians, in the majority of cases, initiate the use of tranquillisers, and decide the dosage and extent of use, their position in relation to the patient is a very powerful one, and their influence on continued usage is also likely to be great, even if that is only perceived in a negative way; that is by lack of encouragement to stop using.

Because taking prescription drugs is seen as appropriate behaviour for women and not generally considered as 'rule-breaking', means of dealing with problem use have only recently been developed. Often the situation will only come to light when caring for children or other dependants is involved and negatively affected.

A reluctance on the part of many GPs and other gatekeepers to services to tackle drinking problems in women often leads to medication being prescribed for their presenting problems, with potentially negative consequences (Sandmaier, 1980). As Reed explains:

> When women visit physicians, mental health clinics or family agencies with complaints of depression, anxiety or low self-esteem as well as the physical and relationship problems that are also likely to be occurring, most often they are prescribed medication. By the time a woman reaches a drug dependence treatment program she is often dually addicted as a result of her previous attempts to seek help. (Reed, 1987, p153)

Prescription drugs and alcohol are a potentially dangerous combination, particularly if a woman is suicidal. In any event, prescribed medication, in some cases, adds an extra dimension to the problems which may be experienced by the substance user.

The question of power imbalance between professionals and their female clients has been identified as an important one. The majority of health professionals in senior positions are male, whose status in the professional hierarchy lends them authority; they therefore have a twofold advantage over women - as men in a society which places women in a subordinate position - and as professional workers. In any case 'caring professionals maintain a social distance from their clients/patients' (Hugman, 1991, p133). This social distance serves a dual purpose, as Hugman explains:

> Maintaining social distance not only provides the professional with power over images of the client/patient, it also serves to sustain the self-images of the professional. (Hugman, 1991, p133)

The professional therefore has the power to define the 'problem' of the individual and set the agenda for 'solutions', while simultaneously maintaining their own integrity in the hierarchy. Hugman also argues that some professionals may use the power differential between themselves and their clients as a means of avoiding 'contamination' from the deviant values of clients. Services which attempt to reduce power imbalances between the professional and client may be less stigmatising for women (or men). However, changes to the traditionally hierarchical approach to service provision can be perceived as a threat to the established order, and therefore may meet with a degree of resistance.

Although research reports are generally critical of the attitudes of health professionals to women drinkers and drug users, there is some evidence of a more enlightened approach and a willingness to promote change amongst some treatment providers (Sargent, 1992; DAWN, 1994). In my study the aims included an exploration of the extent to which alcohol and drug using women, in their attempts to seek help for their problems, are influenced by professional attitudes towards them.

Service Orientation: 'A Cartoon In Sexism'?

Criticism has been made of treatment provision for women drug users and drinkers which reflects stereotypical views of female clients, and perpetuates imbalances of power between professional worker and female client. For example, women who enter formal alcohol and drug services tend to remain in treatment longer than men; a phenomenon attributed in part to male professionals' sexual curiosity towards their female clients (Beckman and Amaro, 1984). Furthermore it is argued that service providers:

> ...have neglected to meet women's needs by responding to women as though their needs were the stereotypic, traditional ones. Consequently, employment issues, problems of living alone, single parenthood, and the skills of self-sufficiency and assertiveness have been underplayed. (Colten and Marsh, 1984)

Although women are less likely to have educational qualifications or employment skills on entering rehabilitation, their need to develop such skills is low on the service agenda in many instances (Marsh, 1982). In addition, treatment goals may be oriented towards successful functioning in traditional gender roles. An example of this type of gendered arrangement in treatment was provided by a worker in a drug rehabilitation unit in London.

> There appeared to be an on-going struggle at some London rehabilitation centres where life was described by one worker as 'like a cartoon in sexism'. The expectation in three houses of one foundation was that residents would model themselves on the behaviour of the house parents. In each house men occupied the highest positions and therefore the model was essentially patriarchal. (Sargent, 1992, p166)

Research suggests that within treatment agencies women may experience negative reactions from others, particularly if their substance use, such as illegal drug use or problem drinking, is negatively sanctioned. For example:

> ...women's experiences within treatment centres are coloured by the stigmatising attitudes towards women's abuse of alcohol held by other drinkers as well as by some of the helping agents. (Thom, 1984, p38)

When women are outnumbered by men in a treatment facility, which is frequently the case with regard to alcohol and illegal drugs, this type of reaction may be particularly noticeable. Commentators have suggested that if the more powerful (male) group in terms of status and power takes precedence in treatment situations then women may suffer various types of harassment (Reed, 1987). I was concerned to discover in my research, therefore, the extent to which women currently in alcohol and drug treatment are affected by aspects of minority status (if indeed they are in a minority), and whether differences in status and power between male and female clients remain significant factors for them.

Service Options

Service options open to women necessarily affect their willingness to consider entering treatment and completing a programme. For example, many agencies do not make separate provision for women, and childcare facilities are scarce. Although the majority of male and female staff questioned in Sargent's (1992) study of agencies for drug users in London, Sydney and Amsterdam, for example, recognised the special needs of women users, only a minority of agencies had developed such facilities. Of the 331 drug and alcohol agencies (of a total of 895 initially contacted) responding to the survey by DAWN (1994) only 12% had a crèche or nursery available in 1992, compared to 15% in 1990, while only 4% of residential agencies surveyed were able to accommodate children. It is disturbing that these facilities actually appear to be in decline. This may be one explanation why few women with children attend alcohol treatment services.

On a more positive note, specialist services for black women increased from 7% in 1990 to 20% in 1992, while services for women from other ethnic minorities also improved from 3% to 9%. More female counsellors are becoming available, (in 94% of agencies in 1992 compared to 79% in 1990); however the availability of women-only sessions has declined, and services for lesbian women remained static (DAWN, 1994). For women with disabilities, specialist services are scarce, only 7% of agencies taking part in the survey provide such a service, while access for wheelchair users is difficult in some agencies.

Treatment agencies seem to be increasingly recognising the needs of younger women; for example specialist services for women under eighteen had increased from 13% to 40% between 1990 and 1992. In contrast only 7% of agencies contacted by DAWN provide a specific service for older women. Outreach, home visits and telephone advice are being developed by some agencies, as is outpatient and community detoxification. These types of services are vital to those who find attending clinics or counselling sessions difficult because of their family or other responsibilities. However, as the agencies who completed DAWN's questionnaire in 1992 only represent around 37% of the total number of such agencies in England and Wales, the overall situation may not be as positive as these statistics suggest. In addition, availability of services for women is affected by geographical location, and services for minority groups are more likely to be found in large urban areas.

Conclusions

In this chapter I have discussed a number of the factors identified by research as influencing formal help-seeking by women. What is certain from the existing evidence is that the barriers to treatment for women in need of professional help are complex.

Research indicates that women substance misusers often express feelings of guilt, and may make efforts to conceal their problems. Although younger women express more liberal attitudes towards female drinking they may experience greater family and societal disapproval, which again may prove a disincentive to help-seeking. The extent to which these factors remain relevant to women problem drinkers, however, and whether female drug users are similarly affected, are areas for further exploration.

Whether a woman's substance misuse problems are recognised and addressed often hinges on professional responses at primary health care level. There is evidence that alcohol and drug use can be overlooked by physicians and social workers, or discussion of the issue with the client avoided. A medical approach and treatment of alternative conditions, for example depression and anxiety, can mask the true nature of the problem, and also, in some cases, lead to dependence on prescription drugs. Stereotypical views of women held by health professionals may also lend themselves to medical rather than social interventions. Power differentials between professional and female client may therefore affect women's access to services and their experiences of helping agencies. Research concerning this topic is rather sparse, however, particularly where interactions with health professionals other than GPs are concerned.

Alcohol and drug treatment services typically on offer may reflect traditional expectations of women, in their emphasis on home and family concerns, while sexist attitudes on the part of the majority of (male) clients may also have a stigmatising effect on women in treatment. A general lack of research on the topic of service use by women, and the costs and benefits to them of the treatment they receive, however, makes drawing firm conclusions difficult. In the chapters which follow, therefore, I return to these topics, and explore them in greater detail in the context of my study findings.

6 Women Substance Users and Contacts with Health Professionals

Introduction

As agency responses play a direct role in women's help-seeking, in this chapter I consider the responses of health professionals to women with alcohol and drug problems, and the effects of interventions on women's help-seeking, from the perspectives of the women involved.

The medical professional in general, and psychiatry in particular, has been the subject of a great deal of criticism for its responses to women's problems. Feminist critiques centre primarily on two sites. Firstly, medicine is criticised as oppressing women as patients, particularly in exercising control over women's bodies, for example in the use of reproductive technology and fertility control (Williams, 1989; Riessman, 1992). Doctors are seen as influenced in their interactions with women by views of behaviour appropriate to gender (Ettorre and Riska, 1995), and expectations that women's roles within families should ideally be expressed by 'exercising responsibility, self sacrifice and good example' (Williams, 1989, p192). The relationship between female patient and doctor is described as one in which power largely resides with the professional (Roberts, 1985; Pascall, 1997), and in which dialogue between doctor and patient may be inhibited by its hierarchical nature (Dobash et al., 1985). It is argued that while an imbalance of power between professional and client exists whether the doctor is male or female, it is particularly evident in doctor-male, patient-female interactions; characterised as 'asymmetrical relationships' (Fisher and Groce, 1985, p345).

Secondly, the situation of women working within health care institutions has been the focus of feminist attention, with the emphasis on women's relative lack of status and authority (Williams, 1989; Doyal, 1995). From this perspective women in general, and particularly those from ethnic minorities, are seen as the 'handmaidens' of the health-care system (Pascall, 1997).

In responding to theories of male dominance in woman/doctor relationships and within the health professions, radical feminists in the 1960s and 1970s led campaigns for women to regain control over their bodies, and promoted alternative women-only forms of health provision (Williams, 1989). Such provision was intended to challenge existing hierarchical forms of health care and to empower women to help themselves; examples of this type of initiative are well-woman clinics, health centres and rape crisis centres. In the UK, however, the system of state-run health care means that the provision of well-woman clinics, which various women's groups have campaigned for, has often been within traditional medical-led services (Doyal and Elston, 1987), which many feminists see as less than ideal.

A number of self-help groups for women with drug and alcohol problems have emerged, with the emphasis on the therapeutic effects of mutual support (Doyal, 1995). These groups have tended to be promoted by non-statutory agencies, however, and access may depend on geographical location and the availability of funding resources. In the main, therefore, women seeking help for their alcohol and drug problems do so from mainstream treatment services. The type of responses they typically receive are therefore pertinent to their continued willingness to seek formal help. In this chapter, therefore, I consider study participants' accounts of their GPs' attitudes towards them, barriers to open communication between doctors and drug-using or drinking patients, and the effects on access to specialist treatment for women.

Although feminist critiques of the medical profession and the exercise of male power therein have been damning, it should also be recognised that there are benefits for individual women in receiving medical attention. The exercise of medical power is not always seen as undesirable by women patients, for example; as Roberts (1985) argues, the 'magical' element involved in consulting doctors, the belief that they have the answers to problems, may be reassuring. According to one GP interviewed in a study of GP's management of alcohol problems, 'They [patients] expect magic and their relatives expect more magic from you' (Thom and Tellez, 1986, p408). Part of this 'magic' may include the prescribing of alternative medication. However drug prescribing has also been criticised as gendered in nature (Miles, 1991; Ettorre and Riska, 1995). GPs' attitudes towards the prescribing of such medication for women with alcohol and drug problems, and women's feelings about receiving such medication, are therefore discussed in this chapter.

While there is little existing research concerning the attitudes of general practitioners towards women with alcohol and drug problems, Thom and

Green (1996) argue that, 'We know even less about the attitudes and responses to problem drinkers of professionals other than general practitioners' (p206). In this chapter, therefore, women's experiences of hospitalisation and contacts with hospital staff are also described.

Communication with Health Professionals in Primary Care Settings

General practitioners are often the first point of contact for women experiencing problems with drugs and alcohol; their reactions may therefore be crucial in influencing the course of a woman's help-seeking from that point onwards (Waller, 1993). However, their 'index of suspicion' with regard to alcohol problems in female patients may be low. GPs may lack specialist training in dealing with alcohol and drug problems, or have negative expectations of interventions (Thom and Tellez, 1986). The role of general practitioners may therefore be confined to referring women on to specialist agencies.

Women in my study experienced both positive and negative responses from their doctors to their substance misuse problems. Only two women described their GPs as wholly supportive in their attitudes, however. For example:

> It was such a relief that I went to my GP, and I burst into tears. She said, 'Close the doors, you're on the sick'. She said, 'You've been drinking because of your worries'. She's obviously seen it. (Helen, aged 48)

Sue, a problem drinker, also described her GP as 'brilliant' and 'very understanding'. She considered herself to be fortunate, however, in that she doubted whether many general practitioners were as well informed about alcohol problems, as she explained:

> I did have a really understanding doctor, I don't think all doctors are like that. I think doctors should be made more aware of alcohol problems. (Sue, aged 47)

Although Anne Marie, a problem drinker, also described her GP as very helpful, her description of a consultation with him suggests firstly that he was somewhat paternalistic in his attitude towards her, and secondly that he had little confidence in the successful outcome of any intervention.

> The doctor gets mad at me, he says, 'You silly girl'; he's known me for twenty-odd years. He's just fed up with me to be honest; he said, 'I'll never believe that you'll stop drinking'. He just jokes and he says, 'We're going to do this for you now, we'll do it for you, but I haven't got much faith in you'. (Anne Marie, aged 41)

One difficult or unhelpful experience with a doctor could affect women's perceptions of the responses they were likely to receive in future consultations. Audrey, another problem drinker, for example, felt unwilling to discuss her difficulties with her GP, partly because she was embarrassed, and partly because she feared an unsympathetic hearing. Her reluctance to consult him was based on previous experience, as she explained:

> In fact I wouldn't even ask the doctor for a sick note...the first time I went he wouldn't give me a sick note. He said, 'I'm not giving you money to go out and get drunk on; you could be working until you go into [rehab.]'. And I said, 'I don't really want to go and sign on the dole'. He said, 'You want to go along to the DHSS and explain you've got a drink problem'. I went, 'Right', and just left. There was no way I could do that, so I·up a week later and made an appointment to see another doctor. I went and told him and he was all right. But then I didn't go back for ages for another one. I thought they'd say, 'No, sort yourself out'. (Audrey, aged 25)

Audrey's difficult experiences with the first GP left her feeling uneasy about approaching other health professionals, and with an increased reluctance to discuss her drinking. In common with many alcohol and drug using women her self esteem was already low and she felt unworthy of help. Unfortunately her doctor's reaction to her problems simply reinforced that view.

Women using illegal drugs also described experiencing less than sympathetic responses from their GPs. I asked Joanne, a heroin user, for example, how her doctor reacted to her:

> ...the one that I was seeing like 'cause I had have more blood tests and that, he [GP] would just sit and grin; they just look at you like scum, they do. He kept saying, 'You're endangering your life', and, 'Stop taking it'. But it's not as easy, just to stop taking it. (Joanne, aged 28)

Joanne felt that her drug taking was directly responsible for her GP's negative attitude towards her, with the result that her poor self image was further diminished by such encounters.

Long familiarity with a family doctor, which might have been expected to encourage openness in communication, could, paradoxically, be a barrier to open discussion of alcohol or drug problems (cf. Thom, 1986). For example, when I asked Chelsea, a heroin user, if she had approached her GP for treatment, she replied:

> ... no, because I was too frightened to because he's my family GP. I thought if my mum goes to him next week and he sees my mum, and because he's known me since I was little, I couldn't go to him. (Chelsea, aged 21)

Rachel, a problem drinker, found that, although she intended to discuss her difficulties with her GP, on reaching his surgery she became nervous and hesitant about doing so. She overcame this potential barrier by writing down what she wanted to tell her doctor, and handing him the letter.

> I went to see doctor E. because I was feeling most peculiar. And I'd actually wrote a suicide note, and I had taken an overdose, and I'd come round from it and I thought, 'I'm going to have to put my thoughts on paper, in writing'. I knew I couldn't talk to the doctor. So I wrote it down on paper and it started from there, me going to the doctors, him reading the paper, Dr. K. coming to see me. Yeah, that's how it happened. (Rachel, aged 41)

As Roberts (1985) found from her study of women patients attending doctors' surgeries, 'It is one thing to know in theory how to overcome nervousness when going to the doctor's, or to avoid remembering other things we wanted to ask just after we've closed the door. It is another thing once you are sitting in front of the doctor' (p25). Because women are accustomed to taking a subordinate position in such exchanges it may be particularly difficult for them to make their views heard effectively.

Kayleigh (aged 37) felt that her family GP was reluctant to broach the subject of drinking with her: 'He probably thought, well, it's up to me to bring it up, sort of thing. It's not his...it's not to him to mention it to me 'till I asked for help'. Kayleigh felt that the onus was on her to instigate any discussion of what she felt was a difficult topic for both parties. The stigma attached to the use of alcohol or drugs, particularly for women, may therefore inhibit or postpone discussion of a problem.

Challenging or assertive behaviour on the part of female patients was also a factor which affected doctors' responses to them. Women are expected to display deference to members of the medical profession, and be grateful for help and support offered (Barrett and Roberts, 1978). 'Good' patients allow doctors to make diagnosis and treatment decisions; they do not challenge their professional authority (Fisher and Groce, 1985; Roberts, 1985). For example, when Brenda, a problem drinker, asked her GP if she could be referred to an alcohol counsellor, she met with an angry response: 'She [GP] stormed out of the room, came back in and slammed the [alcohol team] telephone number on the desk'.

As these examples illustrate, when communication between female patient and doctor is strained or difficult the process of finding specialist help may be unnecessarily complicated or delayed. Differences in power and status, however, make questioning of doctors' decisions difficult, particularly for women patients (Roberts, 1985; Miles, 1991). The doctor acts as the 'official expert' and the gatekeeper to other services which women may need (Lorber, 1997). In addition to gender, social class and race also affect the extent of explanations given to patients regarding doctors' decisions; for example, in doctor/patient interactions explanations concerning treatment are least likely to be given to working-class patients. Cultural and language difficulties experienced by women from ethnic minority groups may also inhibit information giving (Miles, 1991).

From this evidence, I would argue that the 'normal' power imbalance between doctor and female patient is exaggerated by women's status as problem drinkers or drug users. Women whose doctors are unsympathetic towards them, or whose attitudes are negative or condescending, may face additional barriers to recognising problems as drink or drug-related and finding appropriate treatment, while traditional attitudes of deference towards health professionals also inhibit open communication between doctor and female patient. Access to treatment is also affected if GPs view women's attempts at assertiveness negatively.

Prescribed Medication (or 'Just Keep Taking the Tablets')

Women are approximately twice as likely as men to receive prescriptions for minor tranquillisers and antidepressant drugs from their primary care physicians (Hohmann, 1989; Ashton, 1991; Ettorre and Riska, 1993, 1995). While the total prescriptions of tranquillisers fell during the 1980s gender differences remain constant (Miles, 1991). The likelihood of receiving such prescriptions increases with age; for example, in the UK women over the age of forty receive almost 60% of the total of benzodiazepines prescribed (Ashton, 1991).

The majority of women in my study had at some time been prescribed minor tranquillisers or antidepressants, either to assist them reduce their alcohol consumption, or in response to depressive symptoms. While some women were satisfied with this approach, others had misgivings, as one young woman explained:

> I've seen the GP. His answer to it is, 'Here's some sleeping tablets, try and get some sleep'. And I took 'em for three days and I threw them away. I don't want to get off one drug and start on another. (Ali, aged 20)

Ali's concern was mainly about becoming doubly dependent on both alcohol and sleeping pills (cf. Gomberg, 1993). Although she was indeed having problems with sleeping she did not see this as necessarily requiring medication. There was resistance, therefore, on the part of some women to the idea of taking prescribed drugs for their problems. Initial reluctance to using prescribed drugs often diminished, however, as problems with alcohol or depression became more entrenched. Audrey, for example, described her reaction to being offered antidepressants by her GP:

> I was against taking them at first, but then I had no choice. I was twenty-one; I was desperate for a change in the way I felt. I said, 'I want some now'. (Audrey, aged 25)

A common criticism of the prescribing of psychotropic drugs to women is that doctors are overly enthusiastic in using them in the treatment of alcohol problems. Plant (1997) suggests for example, that since it is well established that female problem drinkers are also prone to depression the assumption by doctors is that, 'Since she is bound to be depressed we will start her on antidepressant medication right away' (p210). By seizing on depression as a curable condition the doctor's approach chimes with the disease concept of 'alcoholism', which as Burman (1994) notes, 'evokes images of a dependent sick role with wellness being under the control of medical or mental health professionals' (p124). By focusing on medical solutions to problems, to the exclusion of other influences, social factors are effectively obscured (Mowbray, 1985; Sargent, 1992).

Some doctors were simply unaware that their patients, whom they were treating for depression or anxiety, were in fact drinking heavily. As Smith (1992b) noted, in her study, 'Female alcoholics (sic) often failed to inform their GPs of a drinking problem and GPs often failed to ask' (p6). Explanations for women not discussing problems with alcohol and drugs with health professionals are varied; however embarrassment is undoubtedly an important factor in many cases. Mary, for example, in common with other women, simply failed to mention her drinking habit to her GP and 'got away with it'. When her problems eventually came to light however, it appeared that little had changed in practice.

> The only thing that's changed is she [GP] now says, 'Now how about the drinking?', every time I go to see her [laughs]. (Mary, aged 39)

Mary continued to receive medication for her depressive symptoms; she also continued to drink heavily on occasion. Although some GPs were aware of potential problems and monitored their patients' drug usage, others were willing to allow women to obtain repeat prescriptions of tranquillisers and antidepressants, with few, if any checks. For example:

> I say I used to get the repeat prescription every month, even to the day. Some days I wouldn't take any tablets, I'd leave them all, and then one day I'd take about 40 all at once. I hated myself like that. The kids would be coming home from school finding me collapsed in the hall, I'd be absolutely out of it. I've been through a lot really. (Rachel, aged 41)

For some women, particularly those who were prone to self-harm, the prescribing of medication, such as minor tranquillisers, for their problems could lead to difficulties; for example, the threat of overdose (cf. Lex, 1991). Awareness of the risks involved varied between doctors, however, as one woman's experience illustrates:

> They had me on Librium; they used to give me no more than six Librium at a time. But they've got a new doctor on and I phoned up for a prescription and she gave me sixty [laughs]. But I had to go to the health centre, it was just before I came here, and she spied [saw] them in my bag and took them off me. And I also had another bottle of tablets, and she took them off me too. (Jenny, aged 49)

There was evidence in my study, therefore, of some doctors' resistance to prescribing medication to female problem drinkers and drug users if they suspected misuse. This type of response was particularly evident in relation to the younger group of chaotic alcohol and drug users in the study. Chelsea, a heroin user, for example, was unable to persuade her doctor to prescribe Valium (a minor tranquilliser). I asked her:

> *You mentioned taking Valium, was that prescribed, or was that from elsewhere?*

> I got that on the streets. I tried to go to my doctor for ages for that though, he wouldn't give it me, so I just got that on the streets. (Chelsea, aged 21)

Methadone: The Pros and Cons

Women in withdrawal from heroin often find methadone a useful substitute. Although its prescribing remains controversial, methadone can be helpful to heroin users attempting to regularise their lifestyles, both in terms of benefits to health, and in reducing criminal activities (Parker and Kirby, 1996). However, GPs may be reluctant to become involved in prescribing for drug users (Waller, 1993).

Three women in the study had received methadone from their GPs and three from community drugs teams (all the heroin users in the study). There were some problems evident with regard to dual dependency however, as one heroin user's comments illustrate:

> I ended up going to the doctors and getting a methadone script. I think that lasted two days, and I ended up using both [methadone and heroin]. (Emma, aged 24)

Similarly:

> I got my methadone the first day; it was like, 'I'll just take gear [heroin] today and I'll take my methadone tomorrow', and to be honest it just made it worse because then I had two habits. Because methadone, I think it's worse than gear, methadone. It's horrible stuff, it's really bad to come off, really bad. Gear's bad enough but methadone's terrible. (Lauren, aged 23)

Although these criticisms were voiced, however, for those women in my study who were keen to obtain a prescription (the majority), resentment was expressed at doctors' refusal to prescribe methadone, or attempts to enforce a reducing dose. For example:

> ... my doctors won't prescribe it [methadone]. They want you to come off it but they'll say, 'What are you doing all those days when you're high?' To them we're probably hopeless cases. You know? But I had a doctor

> who prescribed the drugs at the clinic in B; he was like saying, 'You
> need to get lower on your methadone', stuff like that. (Joanne, aged 28)

'Respectable' Women and 'Junkies'

Differences in doctors' attitudes to prescribing alternative medication to
women may be linked to the hierarchy of 'good drugs', and 'bad drugs'
identified by Elizabeth Ettorre (1992), in that tranquillisers are seen as
largely benign in their effects (and therefore suitable for women), while
methadone, in its role as heroin substitute has undesirable associations with
deviant lifestyles and 'street life'. Lauren, for example, pointed out what she
perceived as a lack of sympathy amongst health professionals with drug
users as a group.

> I used to say to them [community drugs team], 'Look I work, and I can't
> get to the chemist, I go to work at ten past eight and I can't get to the
> chemist. What am I supposed to do? Go to work rattling [in
> withdrawal]?' They tell you to get up off your backside and get a job and
> start getting a normal life. (Lauren, aged 20)

Methadone, despite being a prescribed drug, is closer to the 'bad drug' end
of the spectrum, which places it in a sphere inhabited by 'junkies'; by
definition women who are 'hopeless cases'. In contrast concern over
tranquilliser use only arises when it is seen as in danger of 'abuse' by
women. The monitoring of alternative medication, therefore, may depend on
the doctor's view of his or her patient as responsible and respectable, or as
dangerously out of control.

There are also differences between women, however, in what their
expectations are of health services in general, and specialist alcohol and drug
services in particular. There are women who are keen to obtain 'substitute
drugs' from their GPs or community drugs teams, and those who prefer to
find other methods of coping. In an apparently paradoxical situation some
women both solicit the prescription of methadone, and simultaneously
express concern over dual dependency. To explain this phenomenon a
community drugs team leader described how he saw his clients falling
broadly into two main groups in their requirements of alcohol and drug
services.

> What we tend to find is there'll be one group of people coming forward
> for medication - substitute drugs, and you've got another core coming

forward because their life is becoming chaotic, or falling apart because of use. So some people are coming to you for more of what they're having, and some people are coming to you for counselling - to try to put their lives straight.

Experiences of Hospitalisation

The majority of women in my study had been hospitalised or had contacts with hospital casualty departments in connection with their drinking or drug use, either with associated physical problems, or more frequently for psychiatric treatment (mainly detoxification). In previous research around half of GPs involved in treating patients with alcohol problems used hospital referrals as their basic treatment strategy (Thom and Tellez, 1986). The first case described is that of a young heroin user, Joanne, who had a 'bad' injection and subsequently became ill. Her mother was concerned about her welfare, and wanted her to go to the local hospital accident and emergency department. However, Joanne had attended on a previous occasion and was reluctant to return. She explained:

> I didn't want to go because I knew that they'd say, 'Well it's your own fault, it's self inflicted'. I went to the hospital and the doctor were saying, 'Well it's your own fault', so I just walked off. My mum were saying, 'Joanne you've got to do that', and I said, 'Mum, I'm not having that, he doesn't know what it's like to be addicted to something. He's a doctor, he's meant to understand'. It's not like you like being a drug addict; you just get that far deep, you feel like you're at the bottom of the pit and you can't get yourself out. (Joanne, aged 28)

When women were in need of detoxification they were most frequently allocated beds in general psychiatric units, which deal with different types of mental disturbance. This was often perceived as stigmatising by drinkers and drug users, who do not necessarily perceive themselves as mentally ill (Thom and Tellez, 1986; Smith, 1992b). As Lucy, a drinker and drug user, explained:

> From then on it was right downhill, worse than ever, and they took me to the psychiatric department which also deals with detoxes and that. There was nobody normal in there. There was only me doing a detox, everybody else was in there for other problems, so it was quite frightening. And after I'd done the detox they kept me in, they just thought I was really ill. They agreed to let me out after six weeks. 'Please let me out. I'm going

> to crack if you don't let me out of here'. I was in the house cutting myself
> and taking tablets and slashing my stomach with scissors and stupid
> things, bleeding. They arrested me again, yet again, I was always waking
> up in the cells. They arrested me and took me back to the place and said,
> 'If you don't stay here they'll section you'. So I agreed to stay and they
> put me on medication and everything. (Lucy, aged 33)

As Lucy explained she was under some degree of coercion to remain in the
psychiatric unit. This was also the case for Jenny (aged 49), who was
arrested and detained in alcohol detoxification, prior to entering
rehabilitation. Whether or not she was sectioned under the Mental Health
Act is unclear, but by her account she felt under duress to comply with
hospitalisation. While either Lucy or Alice could be perceived as a danger to
themselves and therefore in need of hospitalisation for their own protection,
their experiences of detoxification were unpleasant and occasionally
frightening. Part of the problem was that of feeling, as problem drinkers or
drug users, they were simply in the wrong place. Veronica, a drinker and
amphetamine user, also explained her feelings of displacement, on finding
herself detained in a psychiatric hospital.

> I remember one time waking up with a needle in my arm. I remember
> thinking that I was just in hospital and that I'd done something to
> myself, like I'd had an accident, but I was actually in a locked ward in ...
> psychiatric hospital, and it was more of a shock than anything. And of
> course I was still in denial you see, I was still sort of saying I didn't have
> a drink problem. I didn't realise I had a drink problem, I just thought I
> was a hopeless case. And they put me in this locked ward with other
> alcoholics and I was absolutely outraged, because I felt better than them
> because I wasn't an alcoholic. (Veronica, aged 32)

For Sue, a voluntary patient, however, it was not the proximity of other
patients in the psychiatric unit who presented the difficulty, it was the
reluctance of the staff to engage with alcohol problems. Again, as she
explains, she was admitted to a general psychiatric ward.

> There's no facility for detox there, like most hospitals. I was in there for
> two weeks. The staff just don't understand...they'd no time for you, an
> alcoholic, just give you your pills and that's it. And that is not just my
> opinion, that's other people's opinions that have been in the same
> situation. They are just holding you until you can be passed onto someone
> else. I mean the patients didn't bother me at all, but the staff did. You
> were just there to be given pills, and that was it. (Sue, aged 47)

The issues of power and control evident in women's interactions with health professionals may be magnified in an impersonal hospital setting, where arguably women are more vulnerable to the exercise of medical power. In this study Anne Marie's case stands out as an illustration of the most extreme example of stigmatising attitudes on the part of hospital staff. The responses of health staff to her, when she was admitted for what was ostensibly a physical problem, were unsympathetic at best, and bordering on the callous at worst. She explained:

> ...my back seized up in the bath; they phoned me an ambulance, they took me to hospital, they did all these tests to test my reflexes, and they couldn't find anything wrong. I really felt angry because I had had a drink; I did smell of drink but they just didn't want to know. They thought I was putting it on. I couldn't explain anything to them because they just didn't want to know. (Anne Marie, aged 41)

Because Anne Marie was admitted to hospital smelling of alcohol her physical pain was dismissed as psychosomatic and she was threatened with admission to a psychiatric hospital.

> The sister on the ward said I'd serious psychiatric problems. She was quite abusive to me really. I got so bad that I stopped eating. I wet my bed on purpose, because I just felt helpless, nobody would believe in me. I thought, 'They think I'm mental; they think I'm making it all up'.

Finally, after several weeks of such treatment, when Anne Marie's back was scanned she was found to be in need of an operation. Unfortunately she has subsequently suffered painful after effects, which she suspects may have been exacerbated by the delay in appropriate treatment when doctors thought she was 'putting it on'.

Conclusions

In this chapter I highlight the importance of primary care services, particularly GPs, as many women's first (and often only) point of contact with formal health services. As women drug users and problem drinkers experience additional barriers to help-seeking such involvement takes on additional importance.

A number of barriers to open discussion between health professional and female client were identified. On the women's part, embarrassment, nervousness, lack of confidence, low self esteem, consciousness of stigma, familiarity with a family practitioner, and past negative experiences are all indicated as inhibiting their willingness to consult GPs concerning alcohol and drug problems. On the part of doctors, negative expectations of interventions, negative attitudes towards alcohol and drug users, and stereotypical views of how women should behave, all influence open communication with female patients, and their access to specialist services. The ability of women to negotiate their needs is affected not only by gender, class and race, but also by their deviant status as substance misusers. Where doctors are sympathetic and knowledgeable about drinking and drug use, and about specialist services, they fulfil a valuable role in facilitating treatment, and encouraging women to make the best of what services are available to them. However, the effect of contacts with health professionals and treatment services may not be experienced by women as positive. For example:

> The potentially repressive aspects of treatment-type services are apparent in the power relationships between women and the medical profession and in the medicalisation of women's problems and solutions. Here one is reminded of the historically powerful role of the medical profession in defining 'normal' femininity within the boundaries of monogamous heterosexual sex and reproduction. (Dorn, James and Lee, 1992, p92)

Although the foregoing quotation is extracted from a report on criminal justice issues, in relation to women, HIV, and drugs, where the repressive elements of medical practice are most likely to be in evidence, it is also, I would argue, pertinent to a discussion of women's contacts with health professionals in general.

There was some evidence in this study of a lack of consistency in the monitoring of prescription drugs. Where resistance to such prescribing existed it was generally connected with suspected misuse, either of minor tranquillisers or methadone. However, the type of controls associated with increased awareness of such risks were not uniformly applied. For example, chaotic drinkers or drug users were most likely to meet with opposition to prescribing alternative drugs from their GPs. However, substitute medication can be a useful tool in helping women stabilise their lives, used in a supportive context. Specialist alcohol and drug staff may be able to play a role here in advising and supporting GPs in their attempts to help women substance users (cf. Waller, 1993). Co-operation and liaison between community health providers can increase knowledge on the subject, and reduce both negative attitudes towards substance users and negative expectations of interventions. Those women wishing to effect changes in their lives through counselling support, and not simply seeking a 'quick fix', could then be referred on to specialist agencies before reaching crisis point.

Those women in my study who had been hospitalised for their problems often found themselves in general psychiatric units. There were criticisms of the unsuitability of such units and the type of treatment on offer for women with specific alcohol and drug problems, or with dual diagnosis with a mental health problem, which merit further investigation. Evidence from this study also indicates that stigmatising attitudes on the part of hospital staff to women who use alcohol and drugs are, unfortunately, not consigned to history.

An unsympathetic or stigmatising response, particularly in the early stages of help-seeking, may have lasting implications for women's willingness to approach and confide in health professionals about their problems. If women are to make the fullest use of the support systems which are in place then such barriers to communication must be overcome. At all stages of treatment, from GPs to hospital staff, illegal drug users and younger chaotic alcohol and drug users tend to receive the least sympathetic responses. Considering that these are (with some notable exceptions) women with the most severe physical and psychological problems, such findings are disturbing.

An alternative approach, however, would be to suggest that conventional treatment strategies for women alcohol and drug users require a radical rethink, not only in terms of the type, quality and range of services, but in questioning whether interventions informed by a medical perspective are at all relevant to women users. It may be that generalist services for women in crisis, which take an holistic view of women's lives, in contrast to a medical one, may be of more practical benefit to women. Access to such services is, however, severely limited at present. In the following chapter, therefore, I consider women's experiences of mainstream drug and alcohol treatment services.

7 'It's Different to Come Here as a Woman': The Benefits and Costs of Treatment

Introduction

Women delay seeking treatment for drug and alcohol problems to a greater extent than men, it is suggested, with adverse consequences for their physical and mental health. Hence, women's use (or non-use) of treatment facilities should be regarded as a major topic of concern; one which has received only sketchy attention in the past. One of the aims of my study, therefore, was to document the benefits and costs experienced by women entering residential drug and alcohol treatment, from their own perspectives.

The first part of this chapter focuses on the benefits of treatment reported by women, which include increased self esteem and independence, the development of support systems and improved social networks, and feeling safe. These categories relate to social and psychological functioning and have been adapted from a study by Chiavaroli (1992), of individuals with a history of sexual abuse in treatment for substance use, which utilised particular criteria as a means of measuring progress towards recovery goals. The costs of treatment which women described, in addition to problems with childcare, relate primarily to women's minority status in agencies - particularly concerning relationships with male service users, mixed groupwork, communal living and the gendered use of space.

There are two main approaches to providing alcohol and drug services for women. One is to support women's access to mixed-sex services; the other is to provide specialist women-only services. Neither approach is wholly problem free. A report of an Australian national survey on the characteristics of women with alcohol and other drug problems concludes that at present:

> ...the lack of research means that there is little evidence available to legitimate the development of specialist services for women, so that decisions regarding the funding of services for women may be based on

economic considerations rather than best practice. (Swift, Copeland and Hall, 1996, p1149)

In the second part of this chapter, therefore, I explore strategies for reconciling the benefits and costs of treatment for women, and outline the advantages of screening for physical and sexual abuse, and the merits of specialist women-only agencies, and women's groups within mixed-sex agencies.

The Benefits of Treatment

Self-Esteem and Independence

The type of benefits experienced by women in alcohol and drug rehabilitation are often concerned with aspects of psychological functioning; for example in improving levels of self-esteem. The opportunity to develop previously lacking personal attributes such as self confidence is particularly welcomed, as one woman explained:

> I've got my confidence back, even though I am a quite confident person. I feel maybe I've looked a bit deeper into myself and I feel I'll be able to handle things a lot better, just ordinary things. Not always my alcohol problems, but with life in general. (Brenda, aged 49)

For many women entering rehabilitation, whose lives had previously centred around drinking or drug use, and whose self esteem is consequently diminished, regaining a measure of self confidence is a major step towards recovery. They are encouraged by staff to take on practical tasks in agencies, such as cooking, cleaning, shopping, gardening, and helping new residents to become established (the exact nature of responsibilities varies between agencies and such tasks are, in general, undertaken by both men and women). The ability to make decisions for themselves, even about such minor everyday matters, increases women's feelings of self worth. For example:

> My self esteem is going back up now and I will not be trampled over like I have been in the past. I will not put myself through it, so my confidence is obviously gaining and I'm not frightened to say, 'No'. Which, before I tended to go along with things, because you're just suppressing them

with the alcohol. Yes, it does change your life; it changes how you see things, how you see other people. (Sue, aged 47)

Regaining the ability to act independently, which for many women had been lost in a fog of dependency on drugs and alcohol, is an important factor in making progress towards recovery (cf. Burman, 1994).

I'm there for me at the end of the day. You've got to have that as well; at the end of the day you are alone. I'm not going to take these people with me and be with them forever. I've got to be independent and do it alone now. You've got to remember that part as well. (Lucy, aged 33)

In common with the majority of women in my study Lucy had a history of violent victimisation; she had lived with an abusive partner and had also suffered rape shortly after the birth of her youngest child. Independence for her meant more than the freedom to live a drug free life; it meant the hope for a different type of future for herself and her children. The support of other clients in rehabilitation was also an important factor, however, for Lucy and for other women.

Community Support and Social Networks

A strong sense of community support in treatment was experienced as beneficial by the majority of women; 'Like a big family, really' (Emma, aged 24). Shared experiences between residents provide common ground for mutual support, and the breaking down of social barriers, as Marjorie explained:

You get a lot back from the others. They seem to know when somebody's down, they try and sort of buck you back up. There's always somebody you can talk to, apart from the staff that is; you can go and talk to the staff any time. (Marjorie, aged 43)

Decreases in the level of social isolation experienced by many women (cf. Rhoads, 1983), and corresponding increases in social networks, are therefore positive factors of rehabilitation for many women. Anne Marie, for example, described the changes she experienced as a result of a stay in alcohol treatment:

I've changed the way I think in some ways. I'm not going to stay in the house to please somebody else. I'm going to go out. I need to be around people. I've been happy since I've been here, I've been happy. I like socialising, I like to be with people. And for a long time I've stayed in the house, I've isolated myself. I've been bloody miserable to be honest. (Anne Marie, aged 41)

However, as I will explain later in this chapter, some of the benefits described by women in treatment may be undermined by certain aspects of mixed-sex services.

A 'Safe' Space

The provision of physical and psychological safety is particularly crucial, especially as many women report ongoing violence in their adult relationships. (Swift *et al.*, 1996, p1148)

One of the major benefits of residential treatment for alcohol and drug users is in providing a valued respite from often chaotic lifestyles, and a safe place to recuperate. When I asked one woman about the benefits of rehabilitation for her, she replied:

Not taking speed and feeling safe. Because it got to the point with my husband, that like I just had to look at him, and not that he was making me do it, I was making me do it myself. I needed time away from him to get myself sorted. (Emily, aged 28)

This type of respite care allows women time to reassess their lives, particularly when drug taking or drinking was a joint pursuit with a partner, or if they had experienced violence. The violation of trust in others experienced by women who have been abused means that their need for physical and emotional safety is paramount (Copeland and Hall, 1992). However, there are aspects of such safety for women which may be negatively affected by mixed-sex treatment, as I explain later in this chapter.

The Costs of Treatment

Childcare - 'The Hardest Decision'

It is perhaps ironic that, while problems with drugs or alcohol are regarded as the responsibility of the individual, and in the main private, personal problems, a woman's primary role in childcare brings her difficulties into the public domain. As within the family women are the main caretakers of children, a primary consideration for a mother on the brink of seeking treatment for drug and alcohol-related problems is the care of her children. If she is in need of a stay in a residential unit, unless there are facilities for children (and these are rare, and expensive) the problem is particularly acute. The immediate threat is likely to be one of losing her children, either temporarily or permanently, if suitable alternative arrangements for their care are not readily available (Thom, 1987). However realistic this fear may be, it is likely to influence her decision, as to admit to a problem can leave her open to accusations of incompetence as a mother, and the possibility of losing custody of her children. Women's caring roles, therefore, make them particularly vulnerable to judgements on the part of health and social service professionals of their competence. As one heroin user in Sargent's study explained:

> You're frightened to go to Social Security saying, 'I need help', because - I had a nice flat and the child looked well - I wouldn't tell them I was a heroin addict because I knew that their attitude would have changed towards me. And then she would have been a child at risk all of a sudden. (Sargent, 1992, p174)

The degree of importance attached to childcare provision for women entering treatment varies according to different studies (see, for example, Thom, 1986; Smith, 1992b; Nelson-Zlupko et al., 1996). In my study, however, women experienced problems in accessing both non-residential and residential treatment facilities. (Of thirteen women with dependent children nine had difficulties.) A young single parent, for example, described problems in arranging care for her son when attending a weekly alcohol support group. When I asked her what changes she would like to see in the service, she replied:

> Maybe a childcare service, because a lot of the parents are maybe single parents, or their husbands are at work, so the mothers who have the problem are stuck with their kids all day. So they have to go running round looking for a baby-sitter of some kind. And I think a childcare facility, even if you've got to pay a couple of pound a week to keep it going, I think it would really benefit. (Ali, aged 20)

Other women in the study contemplating entering residential treatment found arranging acceptable childcare an overriding consideration. An agency manager explained that:

Women find it difficult to come into a facility because they've took on the responsibility for childcare. There's one finds it very difficult now because her mother's looking after her children. And that poses problems. Because people find it difficult to come into rehabilitation anyway. It's very difficult to look into yourself, and establish some awareness of yourself. And yet women have the added dimension of childcare, and what's going on with the children. (Manager, drug rehabilitation unit)

The lack of residential childcare for women requiring alcohol and drug rehabilitation is a continuing difficulty. Few agencies provide residential accommodation for children, however, other than for brief visits (only 4% of agencies taking part in DAWN's (1994) survey of alcohol and drug facilities, for example). Where such facilities do exist the cost can be prohibitive. The type of problem typically experienced in accessing suitable treatment is illustrated by one woman's story.

I went to see a few others [agencies] before I came to this one. One of them you couldn't see your children for six weeks and when you could it was only like one day in a week or once in every two weeks. They could stay for one night. And that's not encouraging for women with a drink problem, leaving the home, leaving the children, it was really difficult. It was the hardest decision for me...(Lucy, aged 33)

Lucy eventually decided to take up the offer of a place in rehabilitation only after her children had been taken into foster care by the local authority. Lack of available and acceptable childcare at an earlier stage, however, meant that this decision had been postponed until her situation became desperate. Similarly for Joanne (aged 28), a heroin user whose family had tried over a period of several years to persuade her to enter rehabilitation, the scarcity of residential childcare for her daughter had proved a major stumbling block.

Local authority social services staff are positively involved in arranging childcare for women undergoing alcohol and drug treatment, and are increasingly willing to do so; a point emphasised by treatment agency staff. There remains, however, a degree of resistance on the part of women drug and alcohol users to the idea of local authority social services becoming involved in their lives, and possibly taking children into care (Rosenbaum, 1979). Conflict is evident between the perception of social workers as the 'soft arm of the law' (Hague and Malos, 1993, p139) in relation to child protection, and their role as providers of support and advice to families. Adele, for example, who had problems finding suitable childcare while in treatment, wished to avoid contact with social services if possible, as her perception of their role in relation to drug using mothers was a negative one.

> I've been offered by social services to help my mum out with day-care and money and things, but I've said, 'Oh no, I'm not having them take my kids away'. That's because of the way it's been for years; that's what people think. They don't do anything to make you think different. (Adele, aged 26)

Adele considered that if she had been offered assistance by social services at an earlier stage in her drug 'career' it might have been useful. She pointed out that although she was registered as a heroin user she had not at any time been approached by a health visitor or social worker regarding her children's care. I asked what type of intervention would have been acceptable to her. She replied, 'To actually interfere, without running in to take your kids away'.

Women leading unconventional and often chaotic lifestyles may have had previous experiences with local authorities (or know of other people who have) which act as a deterrent to their voluntarily making contact regarding childcare. Such negative experiences and attitudes are reinforced by media emphasis on social workers' role in child protection (Thom and Green, 1996). Women with alcohol and drug problems are well aware that society in general is critical of their lifestyles; it is therefore unsurprising that they are reluctant to invite criticism of what many see as their most important roles - as mothers. The type of questions which typically arise in this context were identified by a community drugs team leader. They include; 'If I do disclose a drug problem, and I want help, will it affect me as a parent? Will I be under the eye of social services, and will my children be taken off me?'

The knowledge that in order to access funding for residential treatment from local authorities contact with social services departments is necessary may, therefore, deter women from applying. An agency manager explained that from her experience:

> The majority of people who take drugs are generally working class, unemployed, lower educated people. And those people tend to have an idea of social services that conjures up all kinds of fears. So women with children, as soon as they hear that they'll have to go to social services for funding, they scarper. (Manager, drugs rehabilitation unit)

There are two main barriers, therefore, affecting women with dependent children wishing to access treatment; firstly - the practical limitations in finding suitable childcare facilities; and secondly - negative social reactions to drug using and drinking mothers, which may inhibit contact with care agencies. These factors combine to limit the options open to mothers seeking help for alcohol and drug problems.

Women in the minority

Traditionally, alcohol and drug treatment services were organised with men in mind as the primary user group; when women attend, therefore, they are usually in a minority. In each of the agencies visited in the course of my research women were a minority group, although the percentage of female clients varied between agencies (from 15% to 40%). The costs and benefits for women of attending alcohol and drug treatment agencies are necessarily related to their previous life histories (Bollerud, 1990; Young, 1990). Where these include abusive relationships with men (the majority of women in this study), therefore, questions arise over the suitability of traditional mixed-sex therapeutic settings for women's needs (Downs and Miller, 1996).

For many women in mixed-sex units relationships with men are thrown into sharp relief. Although I would not claim that relationships with male clients, or men in general, are problematic for *all* women in treatment, the findings of my study do suggest that aspects of minority status are problematic for some women. I argue that these problems are evident in three specific areas: relationships with male clients; mixed groupwork; and the use of space in agencies.

'A False Sense of Security?': Relationships with Male Service Users

> The men here treat women in the way they think they should be treated. And the women accept that, because that's the message they got. It can be advantageous as a woman here, but it can also be a disadvantage. (Manager, drug rehabilitation unit)

The positive and negative aspects of alcohol and drug treatment for women in mixed-sex agencies are influenced by prevailing gender relations in society. There is a conflict for women in treatment, for example, between developing self-esteem and independence, and the desire for protection; a conflict which is crucial in the early stages of rehabilitation. As one unit manager explained:

> I think it's different to come here as a woman than it is for a man. With a bit of insight, and a bit of experience behind me, I know it's different to come here as a woman. In one sense you can be filled with a false sense of security, because you're surrounded by all these people that want to protect you. And on the other side of the coin it can be very difficult to establish an identity and some independence. Because there's all these people that are wanting to do things for you... (Manager, drug rehabilitation unit)

One way in which treatment for women may be undermined is by joining forces with a male client, which is often viewed as an attractive 'escape route'; for example:

> After I'd been here three months I got involved with a lad in here, and then I left, and I regret it so much because I knew then that I wanted to do it [rehabilitation]. (Chelsea, aged 21)

It was explained by one respondent that the male will often do the 'work' of providing illegal drugs on behalf of his female partner (cf. Sargent, 1992; Taylor, 1993). In effect, therefore, it is a more attractive option for women to abandon treatment in such circumstances than it is for men. In this respect women in treatment can be regarded by other clients as 'having it easier' than men (Anglin, Hser and Booth, 1987), in that they can often find a man willing to support them and their habit.

Sexual relationships formed during treatment are generally discouraged by staff as they are seen to undermine attempts to encourage independence and improve self esteem, particularly for women, who are seen as more vulnerable to losing focus on the aims of treatment. Women's degree of vulnerability in such relationships is a matter of debate, however. One agency manager, for example, argued that:

> We're very clear on relationships, people getting into relationships, being vulnerable. But I suppose that's for both sides really. I don't think women are any more vulnerable than men. (Manager, alcohol rehabilitation unit)

Taking into account the histories of physical and sexual abuse with which many women present for treatment, their accompanying low self esteem and powerlessness, and dependence on men economically (cf. Burman, 1994; Long and Mullen, 1994), however, I would argue that such relationships have at least the potential to be exploitative.

Amongst the younger group of drug using women in particular, relationships with male clients in treatment were often difficult to negotiate, as one woman explained:

> I'd like to see many more women in here. Then again, it's a problem, I go to the men instead of the women. It's really hard being a woman in here, because you've got men chasing after you all the time. And I didn't see it like that, I thought they were being friendly. So it confuses me. (Emma, aged 24)

As a result of criticism from other residents and staff about her being 'over-friendly' with male residents Emma felt that she had to monitor her natural impulses, to be more guarded about whom she befriended and under what circumstances. She therefore began to feel lonely and isolated. If the goals of recovery are accepted as, in part, improved personal communication and support systems (Chiavaroli, 1992), then Emma's experience suggests that her difficulties with male residents were at least to some extent detrimental to her progress.

The type of relationships which women dependent on drugs or alcohol form with men can be seen to exist at one extreme on the continuum of 'normal' male/female relationships (cf. Ettorre 1992; Burman, 1994), in that a woman will often be dependent on her male partner to finance and maintain her supply, in return for housekeeping and sexual services (cf. Rosenbaum, 1981; Sargent, 1992). Tolerance of abusive behaviour by female partners often hinges on the continuance of 'bargains' struck; bargains which reflect the economic and sexual inequalities enshrined in the social arrangements of society. Gender relations in treatment, therefore, can be seen to mirror those of society as a whole, magnified by the dimension of drug and alcohol dependence.

Mixed-Sex Groupwork

In the majority of drug and alcohol rehabilitation units taking part in groupwork with other residents and staff is a vital (and often compulsory) part of the therapeutic programme; life stories and problems are commonly shared in this arena. However, taking part in groups with men may be problematic for women in general, and for certain women in particular.

When women participate in mixed therapeutic groups, for example, they may adjust their behaviour to what they see as appropriate in male company. Adele (aged 26), explained that, 'I think I would break down more, and show more emotion, if there were more women in'. She felt that she had to maintain a brave face in front of the men in the group; in effect inhibiting her range of responses. Her reasons were that, 'I suppose it's men's attitudes as well - they think women are weak'. The prevailing ideology was one in which heterosexual masculinity was the norm, which informed ideas about appropriate gender-specific behaviour (Connell, 1987). In a review of the literature regarding such types of treatment for alcohol problems Jarvis (1992) argues that mixed group settings may be more advantageous for male participants.

> Men may find the group setting more amenable because it provides a social substitute for the drinking scene. In contrast, the group setting may have disadvantages for women because of mixed-sex group dynamics or because women feel exposed to social judgement in groups. (Jarvis, 1992, p1259)

Those women who refused to accept their designated supporting role in therapeutic groups could find life difficult, as Alice explained:

> ... you often find in the group meetings because it's so dominated by men, in the ratio of male to female residents, that again you get the old put down, 'Oh it's just a woman, shut up, what do you know, go back to the kitchen'. That's taking it to an extreme but it is that sort of thing, and a lot of them can't actually handle a woman with something to say. (Alice, aged 44)

The problems for women of being in a minority group are recognised by the majority of agency staff, and attempts are made to counteract any negative aspects (for example by including female staff in group therapy where there are few women clients). They are aware that a gender imbalance can make life uncomfortable for women in treatment. Although the staff may be enlightened, however, male clients are less likely to be so; differences in number, status and power are, after all, in their favour.

In rehabilitation units where encounter groups are held, in which residents can vent grievances with each other in a 'safe' environment, some women felt that their behaviour was under greater scrutiny than that of their male peers.

> ... sometimes if we were having a group, you can guarantee me, K. and S. [female residents] are always going to get grouped [singled out for criticism]. Because of what we're doing and 'cause we're girls [we] probably wouldn't get noticed if we were lads. We get noticed more because we're girls, do you understand me? I know I've only been here

four weeks, but since K. come in, every group we get grouped. (Joanne, aged 28)

Joanne explained that because there were so few women in the unit at any one time they were more 'visible' and therefore likely to be the focus of group attention. 'I think if I were a lad in here doing what I was doing it wouldn't get noticed, and I wouldn't get grouped'. As Otto (1981) points out, the effect of being in a minority group for women may be that of 'making their behaviour more memorable and more commented on' (p165). There are parallels to be drawn between the situation of women in drug rehabilitation and women in the criminal justice system. Heidensohn (1991), for example, argues that the relative 'scarcity and novelty' value of female criminals brings its own problems; 'Being an exception is not always an advantage' (p9).

Women with histories of troubled and abusive relationships with men, who are over-represented in alcohol and drug treatment agencies, may feel intimidated in mixed-sex groups. Although there are men in treatment who have suffered sexual abuse, the percentage of women affected is greater (Burnam *et al.*, 1988; Rohsenow, Corbett and Devine, 1988); furthermore the majority of victimised women have been abused by adult males (Downs and Miller, 1996). If, as agency staff suggested, some men attending agencies have been involved in violence towards women (and the link between alcohol abuse and violence amongst males is well documented; see for example, Gelles, 1972; Kantor and Straus, 1989; Dobash and Dobash, 1998), then the problems faced by women in treatment are likely to differ from those of men. Jenny's experiences are an extreme example of the difficulties faced by women in mixed groups where men predominate, and where women are expected to disclose their life experiences. She explained:

...on the notice board was, 'Jenny. at the next meeting will tell her life story'. And I'm going to be very bad here, because I'm going to say exactly what I said then to that notice board. 'No fucking way' [laughs]. I am not saying anything to nae [no] nine men, that's took a psychiatrist months and months to get out of my heid [head]. (Jenny, aged 49)

Women may experience instances of sexual harassment by men in mixed-sex groups, or unwelcome interest in their sexual history (Marsh and Simpson, 1986). Such experiences can reduce the benefits of treatment as respite care; a place in which to feel safe. The mandatory aspect of taking part in groupwork in certain sectors of alcohol and drug services is arguably therefore a deterrent to involvement for some women, particularly those with histories of abuse (Downs and Miller, 1996).

It has been argued, however, that dealing with men in a group context has the potential to be an empowering experience for vulnerable women, for example:

> You see it's quite interesting here, because we also have a lot of men who've been violent. So you can get an awful lot of things sorted out. Women hear about male frustration leading to violence and the men hear about what it's like to be violated. So while you have to be aware of vulnerabilities, and people feeling frightened, and be careful with that, it can be very useful to empower, particularly the women. It helps them work through that, the victim type feelings really. (Manager, rehabilitation unit)

I would question, however, the extent to which the outcome of such group experiences can be predicted or controlled. There is an element of risk attached for the individual, which for some women would outweigh any potential beneficial effects. Downs and Miller (1996) argue, for example, that women who have been victimised in the past need to exercise control over disclosures made in therapy groups. The issue of control is wider than this however; women who use mind-altering substances are subject to a variety of controls, both at a personal and societal level (Holmila, 1991); controls often policed by men.

Power and control are closely linked concepts. Kirkwood (1993) defines power, for example, as 'the sum total of personal and external resources brought to bear on the exertion of control' (p64). Male power over women is perpetuated by sexual and economic inequalities in society, demonstrated in this study by ways in which women's male partners exercised control over their behaviour; for example, monitoring their movements and taking charge of their drug supplies. Connell (1987) argues that, in addition to the ability to influence decision making, force and emotional pressure are crucial aspects of power in gender relations. Many women in my study had experienced physical violence at the hands of their partners, in addition to emotional, verbal and sexual abuse from men; in what Stanko (1994) describes as 'mundane but controlling forms of violence' (p100).

By relinquishing control in group therapy with men women's previous experiences of powerlessness may be revived, with negative consequences for recovery and an increased possibility of relapse. It is difficult, therefore, to reconcile such experiences with concepts of empowerment in mixed-sex therapy.

Communal Living and Gendered Space: A 'Battle of the Sexes'?

In a community setting solitude can be an elusive commodity; as one woman commented, 'There isn't anywhere you can go to be on your own'. While the need for personal space is gender neutral, within mixed-sex drug and alcohol agencies use of space becomes a gendered issue. A number of women, for example, found their preferred activities and use of agency facilities restricted by the predominance of men. Male activities took precedence; men tended to dominate the available communal space, choice of television programmes, games and topics of conversation. For example:

> I don't like sitting in the room where there's all men. They have Sky television and they like watching football on a Sunday afternoon. The big room's booked all afternoon for football, which leaves the wee [small] room. And they're playing cards in the wee room, and the ghetto blaster. I've no option but to go out, and walk the streets as I've done before, or go up to my room, or sit in the kitchen, or sit on the stairs. (Jenny, aged 49)

In Jenny's case what for male residents was experienced as a supportive, caring environment, for her became a sadly isolating one. The minority status of women in treatment meant that, in effect, they had limited power to influence everyday events. A study by Stanko (1994) which examined the strategies used by women in order to 'make themselves feel safe', found that:

> ...some women allow men to choose the television programmes to watch, some cook the men's food preferences, some keep children out of the men's way, some refuse to be in the same room on their own with sexual harassers. (Stanko, 1994, p100)

In other words women take an accommodating role, anxious to appease men, alert to the possibility of male violence. For women in rehabilitation, vulnerable by virtue both of their substance use and in many cases previous abusive relationships with men, the avoidance of confrontation may become an established survival strategy. Women may cope with their relative lack of power by building a 'praxis of compliance' (Connell, 1987, p123). This type of behaviour can be seen as detrimental to progress in recovery; one of Chiavaroli's (1992) criteria for measuring progress, for example, is that of a reduction in 'victim behaviour', defined as 'people pleasing/subservience', or in this case more accurately as 'men pleasing/subservience'; behaviour fundamentally opposed to notions of developing autonomy.

Although agency staff are generally aware of potential difficulties faced by women in these circumstances there are aspects of male-dominated institutions which are resistant to change. The atmosphere of a 'male club' is difficult to counteract, particularly where space is limited. Community alcohol and drug agencies experience similar problems of making space available for women, when the majority of clients are male.

> It's a bit about, historically drug users were always seen as male, or that's how they were portrayed, and I think any service - I'm always conscious of this when I go to the needle exchange - there's lots of men hanging around women when they're using the exchange. And if I were a user and a woman going into that service for the first time, I'd be pretty reticent. Sometimes it's pretty off-putting when you walk into a room at a service and it's full of males. It wouldn't entice you in; it wouldn't entice me in for a start. (Community drugs team leader, female)

A number of women are regular users of these agencies, suggesting that they have been able to overcome these initial impressions. However, varieties of low level intimidation towards women, whether wholly intentional or not, do occur, and may affect some women's willingness to attend treatment. Several women in this study, for example, reported being subjected to sexist comments from male residents.

> We did have a bit of trouble about a week ago. We were talking about sexist comments in the smoking room and that started to get on people's heads and I just stayed out of the smokers' room then. I felt uncomfortable there. It was like it was a battle of the sexes. (Audrey, aged 25)

Incidents involving sexist behaviour were promptly dealt with by agency staff (if they became aware of them), but it is not difficult to imagine that for vulnerable women, survivors of abuse for example, or those new to an agency, such occurrences could prove distressing. Gendered space in agencies, and the atmosphere of aggressive masculinity which prevails in some, may in certain circumstances undermine aspects of physical and psychological safety for women, and reinforce the social isolation which many drug and alcohol using women experience.

Reconciling the Benefits and Costs for Women

Screening for Physical and Sexual Abuse

Women who have been physically or sexually abused by men may find mixed rehabilitation units unsuitable for their needs. One strategy for identifying those women at risk in such situations is screening for prior physical and sexual abuse (Ireland and Widom, 1994; Simpson *et al.*, 1994; Pearce and Lovejoy, 1995; Downs and Miller, 1996).

For such screening to be effective, however, it should be carried out at assessment for treatment or at an early stage of rehabilitation, to ensure that appropriate specialist help is available (Chiavaroli, 1992; Pearce and Lovejoy, 1995). Staff untrained in dealing with such sensitive issues, who lack the necessary expertise and experience, may unwittingly exacerbate the problem (Swift *et al.*, 1996). In a model of treatment for victimised women described by Bollerud (1990), in addition to providing information to women about substance use and victimisation, questioning about sexual abuse was scheduled to take place at intake evaluations for in-patient treatment. Prior to taking part in groupwork women with a history of abuse were also assessed and prepared by a psychologist.

Bollerud (1990) also argues that, 'the issues presented by male and female abuse victims are somewhat gender specific' (p85), and recommends that therapy groups are conducted separately for men and women. In the following section I consider the merits of single-sex arrangements in alcohol and drug agencies generally.

Women-Only Agencies: A Case for Specialist Treatment?

The advantages of separatist women-only services for women with alcohol and drug problems are a matter of debate amongst researchers and service providers. Thom and Green (1996) argue, for example, that the evidence in favour of such provision is at present anecdotal. However, other commentators identify benefits for women in separate services claiming that:

> The provision of a women-only service precludes male sexual harassment and gives women an opportunity to concentrate on their own needs and desires away from their traditional concerns of social approval and the welfare of others. (Copeland *et al.*, 1993, p82)

Specialist women-only agencies attract women from certain groups, who may otherwise have difficulty in finding treatment suitable for their needs.

The advantages offered by women-only facilities for women who have been abused, for example, were illustrated by the experiences of one woman in my study:

> There were so many men in the community, I think I sat on a chair saying, 'I want to go to a women's rehab'. I found it quite difficult; I had a lot of issues around men, and I'd had a lot of abuse from men in my life, sexually and physically, so it was quite difficult. (Veronica, aged 32)

Although later in her treatment Veronica welcomed the opportunity to make friends with men, her first few weeks in the mixed-sex facility were made uncomfortable by their enforced proximity.

An Australian study found that a specialist women's alcohol rehabilitation service attracted greater numbers of women with histories of abuse, women with children, and more lesbian women than a mixed-sex facility (Copeland *et al.*, 1993), in addition to reducing drop-out rates for these groups (Copeland and Hall, 1992). The study found no significant differences, however, in measurement of treatment outcome between women in the specialist unit and those in the traditional mixed-sex facility. The authors point out, however, that although the specialist women's unit was set up with the intention of providing comprehensive gender-sensitive treatment, there was little difference in practice in treatment content between the two agencies; in both cases treatment was based on the 'disease model' of alcoholism and the twelve step programme. Drawing meaningful conclusions from the research was therefore problematic. Furthermore, as random allocation of clients to services is not feasible on ethical grounds, there is the possibility that the women attending the women-only service were those with the more serious problems. It is argued that, from the existing evidence, 'for a variety of reasons it would be unwise to infer that this means there is no benefit from specialist women's services' (Copeland *et al.*, 1993, p89). A research study in Sweden which compared a specialist women's unit for women with alcohol problems and a traditional mixed-sex unit, did find a superior outcome in rehabilitation and social adjustment for women in the separate facility (Dahlgren and Willander, 1989). The researchers concluded that the existence of such agencies could attract women to seek help earlier in their drinking careers, which in itself could improve their chances of recovery. This may be because such services provide a 'less frightening alternative than treatment at a traditional institution' (p503). Other researchers argue that providing a specialist service with a feminist orientation can effectively improve levels of independence, assertiveness and self esteem for women (Nichols, 1985).

It has been suggested that women's specialist units cannot provide a general solution to the problem of women's alcohol and drug treatment; rather they are 'models and places to develop expertise in the treatment of women' (Swift *et al.*, 1996). The success of this approach, however, would depend heavily on the content of such treatment programmes, as evidenced by the Australian study (Copeland *et al.*, 1993); simply separating off women's services and offering the same type of treatment to women as men may not be sufficient to improve outcome. Ideally a treatment environment should be provided which 'promotes, protects and understands women' (Nelson-Zlupko *et al.*, 1996, p58). The availability of separatist women-only services is limited in practice, however. In the following section therefore, I shall consider the benefits of women-only groups within mixed-sex agencies.

Women-Only Groups: Getting Together as Women

Agency staff interviewed in this study were keen to encourage women in residence to support each other in predominantly male environments. One agency manager, for example, described her agency's strategy concerning women's groups:

> They get a lot of attention from the men, and rightly so they feel good about that. In the women's group we try and say, 'Put it in its place; try and put the situation in perspective. Try and remember what you came here for'. We sit with them and say, 'Look, you need to get together as women and try and value yourself as who you are'. (Manager, drug rehabilitation unit)

The ability to 'get together as women' may be restricted, however, where numbers of women in treatment are limited. In one agency, for example, where traditionally there were few women attendees (three at most, or 15% of clientele) the majority of female clients, mainly young drug users, said they would prefer greater numbers of women in residence.

Women's groups, however, may usefully counteract isolation and offer support for those women uncomfortable with, or intimidated by taking part in groups with men (Baily, 1990). Where there were sufficient women in a agency for a women's group to be formed the majority of women also welcomed the opportunity to get to know their own sex; 'The girls that are here now, we do get on' (Joanne, aged 28). At best, therefore, women-only groups offer an opportunity for women to begin to perceive themselves as 'potential allies and resources for each other' (Bollerud, 1990, p85). A study of group interaction patterns, for example, found greater evidence of affection and interpersonal concern amongst women in the female groups than in mixed groups (Aries, 1976).

On a cautionary note, however, it would be unwise to assume that feminist arguments concerning the advantages of women-only groups will necessarily be shared by female service users. One agency manager in the study, for example, described a tendency for staff with social work training to be 'right on' in their attitudes to gender issues, in ways which women clients users did not always appreciate. A flexible approach by group facilitators and counsellors is therefore desirable (Nichols, 1985). Furthermore, some women actively prefer, and seek out, the company of men.

Abused women may also perceive men as providing a type of guardianship, by virtue of their superior status and power in society (Bollerud, 1990). In addition, women in alcohol and drug rehabilitation may have severe, long- standing problems which make relating to other women difficult. Women sexually abused as children, for example, may be hostile to other women, whom they perceive as having failed to offer protection (Zanowski, 1987; Jehu, 1988). Such women may find it difficult to distinguish between helpful and harmful relationships (Butler and Wintram, 1991). Sargent (1992) argues, however, that those who perceive other women as a threat may benefit from opportunities to find acceptance in their company.

Ideally, women's groups enable women to offer each other the type of support which 'empowers them to detach from patterns of dependence on men' (Bollerud, 1990, p85), thus encouraging a departure from the 'dual dependency' experienced by many female substance users (Ettorre, 1992). According to Nichols (1985), women taking part in a alcohol treatment programme in New Jersey, based on a feminist model of individual counselling and groupwork, gained in assertiveness and independence. Within such a supportive context differences between women of age, race or ethnicity, disability, class or sexuality can be explored.

Women's groups, however, are usually held as a supplementary treatment option, not as an alternative to mixed-sex therapy groups, and are often a once weekly event. The advantages of single-sex groups may therefore be diluted by the relative lack of importance assigned to them within an agency.

Conclusions

The essential task of this chapter has been to consider the benefits and costs of drug and alcohol treatment for women service users, from their perspectives. As little research has been conducted on this topic in the UK these findings are important in identifying those aspects of treatment in which the balance of costs and benefits for women could be redressed. The benefits of treatment described by women focus primarily on regaining self confidence and self esteem, increasing independence, and developing communication skills and supportive networks, within a 'safe' environment. Negative factors associated with minority status may, however, threaten the beneficial aspects of rehabilitation for certain women. Gender inequalities in treatment, however, mirror imbalances of power in society as a whole, and may therefore go unnoticed and unremarked.

The issue of childcare for women requiring alcohol and drug treatment is one which has long been a source of concern to researchers and service providers. The tenacity of those debating the topic, however, has not been matched, for the most part, by an increase in provision for children of female alcohol and drug users. The added dimension of childcare, for women contemplating entering residential rehabilitation in particular, is a major factor influencing decision-making. Resistance to local authority social services involvement in arranging childcare is a complicating factor for some women. This is to some extent an image problem for local authorities, but it remains a very real barrier to treatment for a significant group of women.

I argue that gender relations in alcohol and drug rehabilitation agencies are such that women's interests in general, and some women's in particular, may be marginalised. A gendered imbalance of power is most in evidence in relationships with male service users, mixed groupwork and the use of space in agencies. For those women with histories of troubled or abusive relationships with men such situations may reinforce their feelings of powerlessness. Younger women may face particular difficulties, as their 'novelty value' within agencies singles them out for male attention. Relationships formed with male clients have the potential to cause difficulties for women both during treatment and immediately following discharge.

For a substantial number of women, particularly those with histories of abuse, single-sex agencies are an important option, as they provide a supportive, safe environment in which they may be encouraged to gain confidence and a measure of independence. Such agencies should include residential childcare facilities wherever practicable. If women wish to address their relationships with men this could be achieved in the long-term either by linking a women's hostel to a mixed-sex day centre, where women can join the activities as and when they choose; or by providing the option of moving to a mixed agency at a later stage of treatment. For those women identified as particularly 'at risk', by prior screening for physical and sexual abuse, for example, this type of arrangement would provide a necessary degree of protection. The separation of women's services may not in itself be sufficient to improve the experience and outcome of treatment for women, however, if the content of treatment approaches is not also addressed.

Within existing mixed-sex units women's groups are a valuable resource, although the type of group therapy on offer is also important. Research evidence suggests that groups which have a feminist orientation, for example, are successful in pursuing the type of outcomes valued by women (Nichols, 1985). Women service users should also have control over the timing and context of disclosures in group situations (Downs and Miller, 1996); for example, some women may prefer to recount their life stories in an environment which excludes men. In addition I would argue that women's groups should offer an alternative to the confrontational style of many traditional mixed-sex therapy groups. At present the dearth of women's specialist facilities, and the lack of genuine choice between mixed-sex and women-only groups, however, means that choice of treatment is limited both between and within agencies.

Finally, from a strategic point of view, as one community drugs team leader argued, taking into account the way in which service use relates to the broader picture of what women can or should be doing, effecting change requires a 'quantum leap' on the part of society. He described the intransigent nature of the problem as follows:

> I think services in many ways are geared towards males anyway. There's been a lot of talk about it, but I think the reality is it's still very male oriented. I think services do respond to a very male dominated society really. Despite the best efforts of others [laughs]. Even if you become enlightened it's such a major shift of thinking that thirty years isn't enough. Not only are you changing the attitudes of agencies, but you have to change society's attitudes as well.

8 Conclusions: Breaking Out of the 'Vicious Circle'

Introduction

Until relatively recently women drinkers' and drug users' experiences have been largely ignored or misunderstood. Although feminist work, particularly Elizabeth Ettorre's research (1989a, 1989b, 1992, 1994a, 1994b, 1997), has begun to explore their experiences, feminism has had a limited impact on how substance use/misuse is understood and managed. The main aim of my research, and this book, therefore, has been to explore those aspects of the experience of alcohol and drug problems which are specific to women, focusing specifically on those areas of experience where the dimension of gender has the greatest impact. Alcohol and drug misuse is inextricably bound up with issues of gender inequality, both in public and private. A main theme of this book, therefore, is that of power differentials between men and women, both at a personal level, in heterosexual relationships, and within the wider social sphere; and how these affect women's lives as drinkers and drug users, and as 'survivors' of substance misuse.

A Gendered Approach to Drug Use and Problem Drinking

Having first set the scene by placing women's drug use and problem drinking in its social context, the first main topic explored in the book is that of chaos, as it affects women substance misusers' lives. Drawing on evidence concerning links between the development of alcohol and drug problems and violent victimisation of women, literature on self harm, and research concerning the lifestyle consequences of substance use, I demonstrate that chaos in this context is a gendered phenomenon. Many women in my study have histories of physical and sexual abuse, which firstly increase their vulnerability to developing alcohol and drug problems, and secondly exacerbate their difficulties in coping with these problems. Their lives therefore have the potential to become chaotic; physically, psychologically and socially. Evidence from my study also highlights the

117

inter-related effects of these factors (that is victimisation, self harm, lifestyle consequences and stressful events) on women. Thus it is possible to appreciate the unique nature of women problem drinkers' and drug users' life situations. The emphasis on chaos, however, should not be seen as a defining characteristic of all female alcohol and drug users' lives. Elements of control are also evident, exerted both by women themselves, and by significant others.

Control and its gendered dimensions form the second major focus of the book. Firstly, from women's own perspectives I consider 'getting by', or using drugs and alcohol as a means of coping with everyday responsibilities, a strategy common to many female substance misusers. Secondly, I consider how the concept of control is related to 'getting straight'; that is in controlling alcohol and drug use. Both these categories, 'getting by' and 'getting straight' are linked to gendered social relations, and illustrate how the need to be in control of their own lives, and those of others, affects women. However, women are also subject to external controls, both in the public sphere and in the private; their experiences further illustrate the pervasiveness and the enduring nature of the double standards applied to women's behaviour. Family responses to female drug use, and the monitoring of family members' behaviour, are, for example, affected by the dimension of gender. The main agents of control affecting women drinkers and drug users, however, are male partners. I therefore detail the type of strategies used by male partners to retain control of their partners' behaviour, which can be seen to exist on a 'continuum of control'. However, there is more to control than a simple one-way process; women are also involved in striking 'bargains' with their partners, in return for certain social and economic advantages; in addition some women resist the imposition of controls over their lives. As I explain, however, their capacity for effective resistance may be limited by their social position, both as women living in a patriarchal society, and as women who are caught up in the 'vicious circle' of chaotic substance misuse.

Closely associated with the topic of control is that of the influence of significant others on women drinkers' and drug users' problem recognition and help-seeking. The dimension of gender is also pertinent here; for example the degree of autonomy within social relationships which women typically experience is affected by traditional expectations of women, aspects of gender relations, and norms of privacy within families. Women face different barriers to men in seeking help for their alcohol and drug problems, and may reach physical or psychological crisis point before such help is sought. An understanding of the processes which affect problem recognition and help-seeking by women, therefore, is vital as a precursor to identifying potential areas of intervention. For example, women are often reluctant to admit to problems with alcohol and drugs; a reluctance typically associated with their roles as carers of others, or with fears of adverse reactions. Concealment of their problems may be aided and abetted by family members of users, who wish to prevent a problem from 'going public'. My study suggests that a daughter's drug use may be particularly traumatic for parents, and difficult for them to accept. Further research on this topic is indicated, however.

Male partners, particularly those who share drinking or drug habits, are identified as major players in influencing problem recognition and help-seeking on the part of women. The effect of their influences may be twofold; simultaneously depriving women of the protective effects of social support, and exposing them to additional risks, particularly of relapse after treatment (Gossop *et al.*, 1994). I emphasise the predominantly negative influence of male partners on women's problem recognition and help-seeking (although the effects are more notable for drug users), explaining ways in which such influences are perpetuated, and how partners may resist change. Norms of privacy in married or cohabiting relationships, and their influence on women's willingness to seek outside help, are also explored.

Moving on to the topic of women's under-use of drug and alcohol treatment services, my study highlights the persistence of stigmatising attitudes by health professionals towards women who drink heavily or use drugs. The evidence suggests the desirability of further research regarding professional attitudes to female problem drinkers and drug users, GPs' prescribing of alternative medication (particularly in relation to illegal drug users), the outcome of treatment in different settings, and the content of treatment in general psychiatric units.

In the final chapter I identify those areas of experience which affect women entering residential treatment, looking particularly at the personal benefits and costs involved. The main benefits of treatment described by women, for example, are increased self esteem and independence, and improved support systems and social communication; ideally achievable within a 'safe' environment. Less positively, the lack of appropriate facilities for children, particularly in residential agencies, is a continuing problem for many women seeking treatment. Aspects of minority status in alcohol and drug agencies may also prove negative for women and threaten their progress in recovery; these include relationships with male service users, mixed-sex groupwork, and 'gendered space'. I therefore consider the case for separatist treatment arrangements, concluding that women-only agencies are particularly valuable for women with histories of abuse. In the absence of adequate provision, however, women-only groups within mixed-sex agencies may offer an alternative forum for women who wish to develop mutual support systems.

Differences between Women

Key differences emerge between the younger group of drug using, or chaotic drinking and drug using women (aged 35 and under) in my study, and the older group of predominantly problem drinking women (aged over 35), which may be of interest to service providers. Considering chaotic experiences, for example, younger women are more likely to be in, or to have recently experienced a violent or abusive relationship than older women; relationships which often include the sharing of drugs or drinking sessions. A greater number of younger women report experiencing severe physical and psychological consequences of problem drinking and drug use; for example blackouts, high blood pressure, and risks of contracting Hepatitis C. More women in the younger group describe feeling suicidal or experiencing 'accidental' overdose, while self harm, that is deliberate cutting, is also confined to this age group. However the incidence of actual suicide attempts (usually by means of overdose of prescription drugs) is greater amongst the older group of women.

Younger women are particularly likely to adopt the lifestyle of their drug using or heavy drinking peers, often becoming alienated from 'straight' (non-using) people in the process. There is a marked tendency for them to lose contact with friends from non-using circles and to become reliant for help and support from other users, resulting in a type of social withdrawal. Amongst the older group of women solitary drinking is more the norm, and there is a tendency to drift into this pattern. The consequences for both groups of women may be seen as similar, however, in that social relationships on which they can rely for support tend to diminish. The problem of social isolation is especially acute for older women.

Differences in the experience of control are also evident amongst women in my study. While both groups of women display an awareness of negative social reactions to their alcohol and drug use, the impact on younger women appears to be greater. One solution employed by this group of women is to become less socially active and therefore less 'visible', thus avoiding the most severe social consequences.

In negotiations with male partners, that is in 'striking a bargain', younger women are often willing to accept a degree of dependency (and frequently abuse) in exchange for material returns; for example economic advantages and a ready supply of drugs. When such bargains break down, however, some younger women do leave partners; in this respect they appear freer to act than older women, who are more frequently constrained by responsibility for children, lack of economic independence, and the scarcity of viable alternative lifestyles.

It is, perhaps unsurprisingly, amongst the younger women that resistance to control is most evident: strategies include, for example, taking an active role in drug dealing, and stealing to fund a drug habit. Women participating in these activities often feel they command more respect from men by rejecting their expected passive roles. The effectiveness of such strategies tends to be limited however, as such challenges to male authority are often circumscribed by male resistance (including violence).

Younger women in the study are particularly affected by parental reactions to their substance use, with the result that negative reactions from parents and family members, or even the expectation of such reactions, may delay problem recognition. The influence of friends as a factor inhibiting problem recognition and help-seeking is also notable for younger women; while older women are more likely to report friends (where they exist) as a positive influence in their lives.

Younger drug users, and chaotic drinkers and drug users (aged 35 and under), are more likely to be affected by the negative influence of male partners. Crucial factors affecting problem recognition and help-seeking are a lack of social support (identified as a positive influence on psychological health) and accompanying greater risk of relapse, associated with their relationships with male partners (cf. Gossop *et al.*, 1994; Ussher, 1998). In the case of older women, partners generally exert less influence on their behaviour, although positive support for change is often lacking.

Negative encounters with health and related professionals are more frequently reported by younger women (although not exclusive to this group), in particular the illegal drug users. They are also more likely to experience resistance from doctors to the prescribing of alternative medication (usually methadone), or a greater degree of monitoring of such medication than older women in the study, whose use of predominantly minor tranquillisers may be seen as comparatively less 'deviant' (despite the greater risk of overdose amongst this group). The severity of the problems experienced by the younger women in my study in terms of victimisation, self-harm, and the lifestyle consequences of alcohol and drug use, may therefore be further exacerbated by unsympathetic attitudes held by health professionals.

In considering the benefits and costs of treatment for women, there are particular difficulties experienced by younger women in rehabilitation agencies, relating both to their minority status within institutions, and to their relationships with men. Younger women often find relationships with male clients in agencies difficult to negotiate; for example there are problems with being seen as 'over friendly' with men, and of increased attention in therapy groups (associated with the scarcity and 'novelty value' of women in drug rehabilitation). There is also the ever present temptation of joining forces with a male client and leaving treatment, with the added incentive that the male partner might be persuaded to take on the role of drug provider. The benefits of treatment for this group of women, therefore, are particularly susceptible to undermining by factors associated with minority status.

Recommendations

As treatment for women alcohol and drug users may, as the evidence suggests, present specific problems, the following recommendations are offered as strategies for reducing the costs of treatment for women, and maximising the benefits. I would also suggest that differences identified between the two main groups of women in this study indicate that service providers should be aware of their potentially differing service needs, and that wherever possible efforts should be made to accommodate these. The lack of specialist services for older women is of particular concern (DAWN, 1994).

Service Planning and Delivery

- Service providers should be aware of physical and sexual abuse as a potential problem area for women.
- Assessment for treatment should include screening for physical and sexual abuse at an early stage.
- Single-sex facilities should be provided wherever possible, particularly for women from vulnerable groups.
- Service planning should prioritise provision for childcare.
- Specialist training for GPs and hospital staff should include knowledge of the specific needs of female problem drinkers and drug users.

- Community based agencies should be provided, where possible, as alternatives to residential treatment.
- User consultation should be encouraged in service planning, assessment, and delivery.

Content of Treatment

- Women's social networks may require attention; women may be socially isolated, or mixing solely with other substance misusers. Opportunities for co-operation with other women should therefore be fostered wherever possible.
- Women's groups should be provided as *alternatives* to mixed-sex therapy groups.
- Feminist orientated groupwork should be considered as an alternative to traditional confrontational group activities.

Concluding Comments

The experiences of the women described in this book demonstrate the centrality of gender to an understanding of how alcohol and drug use affects their lives, and the opportunities to survive or escape their circumstances. The nature of the problems women experience with alcohol and drugs differ in certain vital respects from those experienced by men; the influences on them are different, as are the choices open to them and the type of interventions they typically experience. Inequalities which many women routinely experience in their lives, particularly (although not exclusively) in their relationships with men, may also be perpetuated by their experiences in treatment.

In bringing this book to a conclusion I am conscious of the feminist dilemma identified by Betsy Thom (1994) of reconciling practical and strategic feminist aims (Moser, 1989); that is in encouraging forms of service provision which are sensitive to women's needs and help them to cope with their everyday responsibilities, while simultaneously critiquing the gender regime in agencies and society as a whole.

Recent shifts in policy towards community-based agencies and away from in-patient facilities for problem alcohol and drug users (Harrison *et al.*, 1996) may be of benefit to some women (although this largely depends on the extent to which such agencies provide accessible 'women-friendly' services). However, for those women with the most serious problems, a group which may include an increasing number of young drug users, intensive rehabilitation will always be a necessary option.

Early feminist campaigns to encourage the provision of separatist services for women (e.g. DAWN and Camberwell Council on Alcoholism Women's Group) have faltered due to funding difficulties, and largely failed to achieve recognition at mainstream policy level. Advances therefore appear to have been piecemeal, although feminist influence has to some extent been incorporated into institutionalised responses to female substance users, in groups such as Alcohol Concern and the Health Education Authority (Thom, 1994). While the earmarking of government funding for specialist services for women appears unlikely in the present policy climate the increasing number of women entering prison on drug-related charges, and/or with a drug habit (a 13% increase in addicted women sent to prison in 1998), may force a change in thinking (Devlin, 1999). The diverting of women into drug rehabilitation rather than prison, through the drug treatment orders enshrined in the recent Crime and Disorder Act, may encourage both a general expansion of alcohol and drug services for women and a rethink concerning women-only options. If, as I have argued, many of the problems of women's chaotic lifestyles are gender-related - for example victimisation, self harm, the lifestyle consequences of alcohol and drug use, and the frequently negative influence of male partners on problem recognition and help-seeking - then more (or less) of the same cannot be a constructive response. Without increasing governmental support for those (few) specialist projects for women which do exist, or alternatively for generalist services for women in crisis, the number of women entering prison with drug-related problems is likely to continue to rise (Devlin, 1999). A staff member at New Hall women's prison was recently quoted as saying that, 'If the government is absolutely honest about dealing with drugs, the three most important things are treatment, treatment and treatment' (Edgar and O'Donnell, 1998, p37).

However, the problems experienced by women who misuse alcohol and/or drugs are wider than those of treatment considerations. As was indicated in the introduction to this book, in a society in which gendered relations, (in a similar way to class or race relations), are characterised by subordination and domination (Hall, 1990) their problems (albeit to a greater or lesser degree) are common to women as a group. The majority of women in my study were living, or had recently been living, within what Ussher (1998) describes as the 'traditional heterosexual matrix', in which power imbalances between partners were a key ingredient, and where women were often physically, sexually, or emotionally abused. Change in the gender order however is an incremental process and 'changing deeply embedded patterns of relationships that have served a dominant group for so long (in this case men) will never happen overnight' (Ussher, 1998, p159). In the longer term, however:

> What is needed is a change in the wider social sphere, empowerment of individual women (and arguably some men) and a reconceptualisation of masculinity and femininity, leading to more egalitarian relationships between men and women. (Ussher, 1998, p159)

There is evidence of some women attempting to 'rewrite the script' in their relationships with men, resisting traditional expectations of them as women. What they lack in many cases however is material support, to assist them in challenging the status quo; and alternative strategies in coping with their problems, other than resorting to drinking or using drugs. The provision of legal, economic and social support for women wishing to leave violent relationships, for example, may help them in breaking out of the 'vicious circle' in which so many women in my study had become enmeshed.

Bibliography

ACMD (Advisory Council on the Misuse of Drugs) (1982) *Treatment and Rehabilitation: Report of the Advisory Council on the Misuse of Drugs.* HMSO, London.

Adler, S., Laney, J. and Packer, M. (1993) *Managing Women: Feminism and Power in Educational Management.* OU Press, Buckingham.

Almog, Y.J., Anglin, M.D. and Fisher, D.G. (1993) Alcohol and Heroin Use Patterns of Narcotic Addicts: Gender and Ethnic Differences, *American Journal of Drug and Alcohol Abuse*, vol. 19 (2), pp. 219-238.

Anglin, M.D., Hser, Y. and Booth, M.A. (1987) Sex Differences in Addict Careers. 4. Treatment, *American Journal of Drug and Alcohol Abuse*, vol. 13(3), pp. 253-280.

Arber, S. (1993) Designing Samples, in N. Gilbert (ed.) *Researching Social Life.* Sage Publications, London.

Aries, E. (1976) Interaction Patterns and Themes of Male, Female and Mixed Groups, *Small Group Behaviour*, vol. 7(1), pp. 718-30.

Ashton, H. (1991) Psychotropic-Drug Prescribing for Women, *British Journal of Psychiatry*, vol. 158 (Suppl. 10), pp. 30-35.

Baily, S. (1990) Women with Alcohol Problems: A Psycho-Social Perspective, in *Drug and Alcohol Review*, vol. 9, pp. 125-31.

Barrett, M. and Roberts, H. (1978) Doctors and their Patients: The Social Control of Women in General Practice, in C. Smart and B. Smart (eds) *Women, Sexuality and Social Control.* Routledge and Kegan Paul, London.

Beckman, L.J. (1994) Treatment Needs of Women with Alcohol Problems, *Alcohol Health and Research World*, vol. 18(3), pp.206-211.

Beckman, L.J. and Amaro, H. (1984) Patterns of Women's Use of Alcohol Treatment Agencies, in S.C. Wilsnack and L J. Beckman (eds) *Alcohol Problems in Women: Antecedents, Consequences and Intervention.* Guildford, New York.

Belle, D. (ed.) (1982) *Lives in Stress: Women and Depression.* Sage Publications, London.

Berardo, F.M. (1998) Family Privacy Issues and Concepts, *Journal of Family Issues*, vol. 19(1), pp. 4-19.

Blume, S.B. (1990) Chemical Dependency in Women: Important Issues, *American Journal of Drug and Alcohol Abuse*, vol. 16 (3 & 4), pp. 297-307.

Bograd, M. (1988) Feminist Perspectives on Wife Abuse: An Introduction, in K. Yllo (ed.) *Feminist Perspectives on Wife Abuse.* Sage Publications, London.

Bollerud, K. (1990) A Model for the Treatment of Trauma-Related Syndromes among Chemically Dependent Inpatient Women, *Journal of Substance Abuse Treatment*, vol. 7, pp. 83-87.

Borkowski, M., Murch, M. and Walker, V. (1983) *Marital Violence: The Community Response*. Tavistock, London.

Bowser, B. P. and Sieber, J. E. (1993) AIDS Prevention Research: Old Problems and New Solutions, in C.M. Renzetti and R. Lee (eds) *Researching Sensitive Topics*. Sage, London.

Brittan, A. and Maynard, M. (1984) *Sexism, Racism and Oppression*. Basil Blackwell Publisher Ltd., Oxford.

Brown, G.W. and Harris, T. (1978) *Social Origins of Depression: A Study of Psychiatric Disorder in Women*. Tavistock Publications, London.

Brown-Smith, N. (1998) Family Secrets, in *Journal of Family Issues*, vol. 19(1), pp. 20-42.

Bryson, L. (1992) *Welfare and the State: Who Benefits?* MacMillan, London.

Burman, S. (1994) The Disease Concept of Alcoholism: Its Impact on Women's Treatment, *Journal of Substance Abuse Treatment*, vol. 11(2), pp. 121-126.

Burnam, M.A., Stein, J.A., Golding, J.M., Siegel, J.M., Sorenson, S.B., Forsythe, A.B. and Telles, C.A. (1988) Sexual Assault and Mental Disorders in a Community Population, *Journal of Consulting and Clinical Psychology*, vol. 56(6), pp. 843-850.

Busfield, J. (1996) *Men, Women and Madness: Understanding Gender and Mental Disorder*. MacMillan, London.

Butler, S. and Wintram, C. (1991) *Feminist Groupwork*. Sage Publications, London.

Carmen, E., Russo, N.F. and Miller, J.B. (1981) Inequality and Women's Mental Health, An Overview, *American Journal of Psychiatry*, vol. 138(10), pp.1319-1330.

Chiavaroli, T. (1992) Rehabilitation from Substance Use in Individuals with a History of Sexual Abuse, *Journal of Substance Abuse Treatment*, vol. 9, pp. 349-354.

Collins, R. L. (1993) Women's Issues in Alcohol Use and Cigarette Smoking, in J.S. Baer, G.A. Marlatt and R.J. McMahon (eds) *Addictive Behaviours Across the Lifespan: Prevention, Treatment and Policy Series*. Sage, Newbury Park.

Colten, M.E. and Marsh, J.C. (1984) A Sex-Roles Perspective on Drug and Alcohol Use by Women, in C.P. Wisdom (ed.) *Sex Roles and Psychopathology*. Plenum Press, New York.

Connell, R.W. (1987) *Gender and Power*. Polity Press, Cambridge.

Connell, R.W. (1995) *Masculinities*. Polity Press, Cambridge.

Copeland, J. and Hall, W. (1992) A Comparison of Predictors of Treatment Drop-out of Women Seeking Drug and Alcohol Treatment in a Specialist

Women's and Two Traditional Mixed-Sex Treatment Services, *British Journal of Addiction*, vol. 87, pp.883-890.

Copeland, J., Hall, W., Didcott, P. and Biggs, V. (1993) A Comparison of a Specialist Women's Alcohol and Other Drug treatment Service with Two Traditional Mixed-Sex Services: Client Characteristics and Treatment Outcome, *Drug and Alcohol Dependence*, vol. 32, pp.81-92.

Dahlgren, L. and Myrhed, M. (1977) Ways of Admission of the Alcoholic Patient: A Study with Special Reference to the Alcoholic Female, *Acta Psychiatrica Scandinavia*, vol. 56, pp.39-49.

Dahlgren, L. and Willander, A. (1989) Are Specialist Treatment Facilities for Female Alcoholics Needed? A Controlled 2 Year Follow-up Study from a Specialized Female Unit (EWA) versus a Mixed Male/Female Treatment Facility, *Alcoholism, Clinical and Experimental Research*, vol. 13(4), pp. 499-505.

Daly, F. (1992) Drug Users on Bail: A Voluntary Agency's Experience, in N. Dorn, B. James and M. Lee (eds) *Women, HIV, Drugs*. ISDD, London.

Davis, S. (1994) Drug Treatment Decisions of Chemically Dependent Women, *The International Journal of the Addictions*, vol. 29(10), pp. 1287-1304.

Davison, S. and Marshall, J. (1996) Women with Drug and Alcohol Problems, in K. Abel, M. Buszewicz, S. Davison, S. Johnson and E. Staples. (eds) *Planning Community Mental Health Services for Women*. Routledge, London.

DAWN Drugs, Alcohol, Women, Nationally (1994) *When a Creche is Not Enough: A Survey of Drug and Alcohol Services for Women*. DAWN, London.

Devlin, A. (1999) On Drugs and Behind Bars, *The Guardian*, March 11, p7.

Dobash, R.E. and Dobash, R. (1979) *Violence Against Wives*. Free Press, New York.

Dobash, R.E., Dobash, R.P. and Cavanagh, K. (1985) The Contact between Battered Women and Social and Medical Agencies, in J. Pahl. (ed.) *Private Violence and Public Policy*. Routledge and Kegan Paul, London.

Dobash, R.E. and Dobash, R.P. (1998) *Rethinking Violence Against Women*. Sage Publications, London.

Donoghoe, M., Dorn, N., James, C., Jones, S., Ribbens, J. and South, N. (1987) How Families and Communities Respond to Heroin, in N. Dorn and N. South (eds) *A Land Fit for Heroin: Drug Policies, Prevention and Practice*. MacMillan Education Ltd, London.

Dorn, N., James, B. and Lee, M. (1992) *Women, HIV, Drugs: Criminal Justice Issues*. ISDD, London.

Dorn, N., Ribbens, J. and South, N. (1987) *Coping with a Nightmare: Family Feelings about Long-term Drug Use*. ISDD, London.

Downs, W.R. and Miller, B.A. (1996) Inter-Generational Links between Childhood Abuse and Alcohol-related Problems, in L. Harrison (ed.) *Alcohol Problems in the Community*. Routledge, London.

Doyal, L. (1995) *What Makes Women Sick: Gender and the Political Economy of Health*. MacMillan, London.

Doyal, L. (1999) Sex, Gender and Health: A New Approach, in S. Watson and L. Doyal (eds) *Engendering Social Policy*. Open University Press, Buckingham.

Doyal, L. and Elston, M.A. (1987) Women, Health and Medicine, in V. Beechey and E. Whitelegg (eds) *Women in Britain Today*. Open University Press, Buckingham.

Eaton, M. (1993) *Women After Prison*. Open University Press, Buckingham.

Edgar, K. and O'Donnell, I. (1998) *Mandatory Drug Testing in Prisons: The Relationship betwen MDT and the Level and Nature of Drug Misuse*. Home Office Research Study 189, London.

Estep, R. (1987) The Influence of the Family on the Use of Alcohol and Prescription Depressants by Women, *Journal of Psychoactive Drugs*, vol. 19(2), pp.171-179.

Ettorre, B. (1989a) Women and Substance Use/Abuse: Towards a Feminist Perspective or How to Make Dust Fly, *Women's Studies International Forum*, vol. 12(6), pp.593-602.

Ettorre, B. (1989b) Women, Substance Abuse and Self-Help, in S. MacGregor (ed.) *Drugs and British Society: Responses to a Social Problem in the Eighties*. Routledge, London.

Ettorre, E. (1992) *Women and Substance Use*. MacMillan, London.

Ettorre, E. (1994a) Substance Use and Women's Health, in S. Wilkinson and C. Kitzinger (eds) *Women and Health: Feminist Perspectives*. Taylor and Francis, London.

Ettorre, E. (1994b) Women and Drug Abuse with Special Reference to Finland: Needing the Courage to See, *Women's Studies International Forum*, vol. 17(1), pp. 83-94.

Ettorre, E. (1997) *Women and Alcohol: A Private Pleasure or a Public Problem*. The Women's Press Ltd, London.

Ettorre, E., Klaukka, T. and Riska, E. (1994) Psychotropic Drugs: Long-term Use, Dependency and the Gender Factor, *Social Science and Medicine*, vol. 39(12), pp.1667-1673

Ettorre, E. and Riska, E. (1993) Psychotropics, Sociology and Women, *Sociology of Health and Illness*, vol. 15(1), pp.503-524.

Ettorre, E. and Riska, E. (1995) *Gendered Moods: Psychotropics and Society*. Routledge, London.

Faupel, C.E. and Hanke, P.J. (1993) A Comparative Analysis of Drug-Using Women With and Without Treatment Histories in New York City, *The International Journal of Addictions*, vol. 28(3), pp. 233-248.

Fisher, S. and Groce, S.B. (1985) Doctor-Patient Negotiation of Cultural Assumptions, *Sociology of Health and Illness*, vol. 7(3), pp. 342-374.

Forth-Finegan, J.L. (1992) Sugar and Spice and Everything Nice: Gender Socialization and Women's Addiction - A Literature Review, in C. Bepko (ed.) *Feminism and Addiction*. Hayworth Press, New York.

Gabe, J. (1991) *Understanding Tranquilliser Use: The Role of the Social Sciences*. Routledge, London.

Gabe, J. and Thorogood, N. (1986) Prescribed Drug Use and the Management of Everyday Life: the Experiences of Black and White Working-Class Women, *Sociological Review*, vol. 34 (4), pp. 737-772.

Gay, P. (1989) *Getting Together: A Study of Self-Help Groups for Drug Users' Families*. Policy Studies Institute, London.

Gelles, R.J. (1972) *The Violent Home*. Sage Publications, London.

Gomberg, E.S.L. (1982) Historical and Political Perspective: Women and Drug Use, *Journal of Social Issues*, vol. 38(2), pp. 9-23.

Gomberg, E.S.L. (1988) Alcoholic Women in Treatment, The Question of Stigma and Age, *Alcohol and Alcoholism*, vol. 223, pp.507-14.

Gomberg, E.S.L. (1993) Women and Alcohol: Use and Abuse, *The Journal of Nervous and Mental Disease*, vol. 181 (4), pp. 211-219.

Gormon, J. (1992) *Out of the Shadows: Stress on Women*. MIND Publications, London.

Gossop, M., Griffiths, P. and Strang, J. (1988) Chasing the Dragon: Characteristics of Heroin Chasers, *British Journal of Addiction*, vol. 83, pp. 1159-1162.

Gossop, M., Griffiths, P. and Strang, J. (1994) Sex Differences in Patterns of Drug Taking Behaviour, *British Journal of Psychiatry*, vol. 164, pp. 101-104.

Graham, H. (1984) *Women, Health and the Family*. Wheatsheaf, Brighton.

Graham, H. (1993) *Hardship and Health in Women's Lives*. Harvester Wheatsheaf, London.

Green, E., Hebron, S. and Woodward, D. (1987) Women, Leisure and Social Control, in J. Hanmer and M. Maynard (eds) *Women, Violence and Social Control*. MacMillan Press Ltd, London.

Griffiths, R. and Pearson, B. (eds) (1988) *Working with Drug Users*. Wildwood House, Aldershot.

Hague, G. and Malos, E. (1993) *Domestic Violence: Action for Change*. New Clarion Press, Cheltenham.

Hall, D. and Hall, I. (1996) *Practical Social Research*. Macmillan Press Ltd, London.

Harrison, L., Guy, P. and Sivyer, W. (1996) Community Care Policy and the Future of Alcohol Services, in L. Harrison (ed.) *Alcohol Problems in the Community*. Routledge, London.

Harrison, P.A. (1989) Women in Treatment: Changing Over Time, *The International Journal of the Addictions*, vol. 24(7), pp. 655-673.

Harrison, P.A. and Belille, C.A. (1987) Women in Treatment: Beyond the Stereotype, *Journal of Studies on Alcohol*, vol. 48(6), pp. 574-578.

Heidensohn, F. (1991) The Crimes of Women, *Criminal Justice Matters*, No 5, Winter 1991, p9.

Hoff, L.A. (1990) *Battered Women as Survivors*. Routledge, London.

Hohmann, A.A. (1989) Gender Bias in Psychotropic Drug Prescribing in Primary Care, *Medical Care*, vol. 27(5), pp. 478-90.

Holmila, M. (1991) Social Control Experienced by Heavily Drinking Women, *Contemporary Drug Problems*, Winter 1991, pp.547-571.

Home Office (1986) *Tacking Drug Misuse* (Second Edition). HMSO, London.

Hser, Y.I., Anglin, M.D. and Booth, M.W. (1987) Sex Differences in Addict Careers. 3. Addiction, *American Journal of Drug and Alcohol Abuse*, vol. 13(3), pp. 231-251.

Hugman, R. (1988) Ethnography and Social Care, *Social Services Research*, vol. 1, pp. 11-20.

Hugman, R. (1991) *Power in the Caring Professions*. MacMillan Education Ltd., London.

Hutter, B. and Williams, G. (eds) (1981) *Controlling Women: The Normal and the Deviant*. Croom Helm, London.

Ireland, T. and Widom, C.S. (1994) Childhood Victimization and Risk for Alcohol and Drug Arrests, *The International Journal of the Addictions*, vol. 29(2), pp. 235-274.

ISDD Institute for the Study of Drug Dependence (1994) *Drug Misuse in Britain, 1994*. ISDD, London.

James, A. (1997) Self Harm: Whose Taboo?, *Asylum*, vol. 10 (2), pp. 12-13.

Jarvis, T.J. (1992) Implications of Gender for Alcohol Treatment Research: A Quantitative and Qualitative Review, *British Journal of Addiction*, vol. 87, pp. 1249-61.

Jehu, D. (1988) *Beyond Sexual Abuse: Therapy with Women who were Childhood Victims*. John Wiley and Sons, Chichester.

Johnson, P. B. (1982) Sex Differences and Alcohol, *Journal of Social Issues*, vol. 38(2), pp. 113-115.

Kandiyoti, D. (1988) Bargaining with Patriarchy, *Gender and Society*, vol. 2(3), pp. 274-290.

Kantor, G.A. and Straus, M.A. (1989) Substance Abuse as a Precipitant of Wife Abuse Victimisations, *American Journal of Drug and Alcohol Abuse*, vol. 15(2), pp. 173-189.

Kirkwood, C. (1993) *Leaving Abusive Partners*. Sage Publications, London.

Koffinke, C. (1991) Family Recovery Issues and Treatment Resources, in D.C. Daley and M.S. Raskin (eds) *Treating the Chemically Dependent and Their Families*. Sage Publications, London.

Koss, M. (1990) The Women's Mental Health Research Agenda: Violence Against Women, *American Psychologist*, vol. 45(3), pp. 374-80.

Ladwig, G.B. and Anderson, M.D. (1989) Substance Abuse in Women: Relationship Between Chemical Dependency of Women and Past Reports of Physical and/or Sexual Abuse, *The International Journal of Addictions*, vol. 24(8), pp. 739-754.

Land, H. and Rose, H. (1985) Compulsory Altruism for Some or an Altruistic Society for All, in P. Bean, J. Ferris and D. Whynes (eds) *In Defence of Welfare.* Tavistock, London.

Lee, R.M. (1993) *Doing Research on Sensitive Topics.* Sage Publications, London.

Lex, B.W. (1991) Some Gender Differences in Alcohol and Polysubstance Users, *Health Psychology*, vol. 10 (2), pp. 121-132.

Lincoln, Y. S. and Guba, E. G. (1985) *Naturalistic Enquiry.* Sage Publications, London.

Long, A. and Mullen, B. (1994) An Exploration of Women's Perceptions of the Major Factors that Contributed to Their Alcohol Abuse, *Journal of Advanced Nursing*, vol. 19, pp.623-639.

Lorber, J. (1997) *Gender and the Social Construction of Illness.* Sage Publications, London.

McDonald, M. (ed.) (1994) *Gender, Drink and Drugs.* Berg Publishers, Oxford.

MacGregor, S. (1989) Choices for Policy and Practice, in S. MacGregor (ed.) *Drugs and British Society: Responses to a Social Problem in the Eighties.* Routledge, London.

Makosky, V. P. (1982) Sources of Stress: Events or Conditions? in D. Belle (ed.) *Lives in Stress: Women and Depression.* Sage Publications, London.

Marsh, J. C. (1982) Public Issues and Private Problems: Women and Drug Use, *Journal of Social Issues*, vol. 38(2), pp. 153-165.

Marsh, J.C. and Miller, N.A. (1985) Female Clients in Substance Abuse Treatment, *The International Journal of the Addictions*, vol. 20 (6 and 7), pp. 995-1019.

Marsh, K.L. and Simpson, D.W. (1986) Sex Differences in Opioid Addiction Careers, *American Journal of Drug and Alcohol Abuse*, vol. 12, pp. 309-329.

Mason, J. (1996) *Qualitative Researching.* Sage Publications, London.

Massella, J.D. (1991) Intervention: Breaking the Addiction Cycle, in D.C. Daley and M.S. Raskin (eds) *Treating the Chemically Dependent and Their Families.* Sage Publications, London.

Measor, L. (1985) Interviewing: a Strategy in Qualitative Research, in R.G. Burgess (ed.) *Strategies of Educational Research: Qualitative Methods.* Falmer Press, London.

Miles, A. (1981) *The Mentally Ill in Contemporary Society: A Sociological Introduction.* Martin Robertson, Oxford.

Miles, A. (1991) *Women, Health and Medicine.* Open University Press, Buckingham.

Miller, B.A. and Downs, W.R. (1993) The Impact of Family Violence on Use of Alcohol by Women, *Alcohol, Health and Research*, vol. 17, pp. 137-143.

Miller, B.A. and Downs, W.R. (1995) Violent Victimization among Women with Alcohol Problems, in M. Galanter (ed.) *Recent Developments in Alcoholism*. Plenum Press, New York.

Miller, B.A., Downs, W.R., Gondoli, D.M. and Keil, A.K. (1987) The Role of Childhood Sexual Abuse in the Development of Alcoholism in Women, *Violence and Victims*, vol. 2 (3), pp. 157-171.

Miller, B.A., Downs, W.R. and Testa, M. (1993) Interrelationships between Victimization Experiences and Women's Alcohol/Drug Use, *Journal of Studies on Alcohol*, Supp. No. 11, pp. 109-117.

Morgan, D. L. (1988) *Focus Groups as Qualitative Research*. Sage Publications, London.

Morrice, J.K.W. (1976) *Crisis Intervention: Studies in Community Care*. Pergamon Press, Oxford.

Moser, C.O.N. (1989) Gender Planning in the Third World: Meeting Practical and Strategic Gender Needs, *World Development*, vol. 17 (11), pp. 1799-1825.

Mowbray, C.T. (1985) A Case Study: Women and the Health Care System - Patients or Victims?, in C.T. Mowbray, S. Lanir and M. Hulce (eds) *Women and Mental Health: New Directions for Change*. Harrington Park Press, London.

Murphy, P.N. and Bentall, R.P. (1992) Motivation to Withdraw from Heroin: A Factor-Analytic Study, *British Journal of Addiction*, vol. 87, pp. 245-250.

Nelson-Zlupko, L., Dore, M.M., Kauffman, E. and Kaltenbach, K. (1996) Women in Recovery: Their Perceptions of Treatment Effectiveness, *Journal of Substance Abuse Treatment*, vol. 13(1), pp. 51-59.

Nichols, M. (1985) Theoretical Concerns in the Clinical Treatment of Substance-Abusing Women: A Feminist Analysis, *Alcohol Treatment Quarterly*, vol.2 (1), pp. 79-90.

Oakley, A. (1974) *The Sociology of Housework*. Pantheon, New York.

O'Connell Davidson, J. and Layder, D. (1994) *Methods, Sex and Madness*. Routledge, London.

Orford, J. (1985) Alcohol Problems and the Family, in J. Lishman (ed.) *Research Highlights in Social Work: Approaches to Addiction*. Kogan Page, London.

Otto, S. (1981) Women, Alcohol and Social Control, in B. Hutter and G. Williams (eds) *Controlling Women: The Normal and the Deviant*. Croom Helm, London.

Pahl, J. (ed.) (1985) *Private Violence and Public Policy: The Needs of Battered Women and the Response of the Public Services*. Routledge and Kegan Paul, London.

Parker, H., Bakx, K. and Newcombe, R. (1988) *Living with Heroin*. Open University Press, Buckingham.

Parker, H. and Kirby, P. (1996) *Methadone Maintenance and Crime Reduction on Merseyside.* Crime Detection and Prevention Series, Paper 72. Home Office, London.

Pascall, G. (1986) *Social Policy: A Feminist Analysis.* Tavistock, London.

Pascall, G. (1997) *Social Policy: A New Feminist Analysis.* Routledge, London.

Payne, S. (1991) *Women, Health and Poverty.* Harvester Wheatsheaf, Hemel Hempstead.

Pearce, E.J. and Lovejoy, F.H. (1995) Detecting a History of Childhood Sexual Experiences Among Women Substance Abusers, *Journal of Substance Abuse Treatment,* vol. 12(4), pp. 283-287.

Perry, L. (1979) *Women and Drug Use: An Unfeminine Dependency.* ISDD, London.

Plant, M. (1997) *Women and Alcohol: Contemporary and Historical Perspectives.* Free Association Books, London.

Raine, P. (1995) Families and Substance Dependency, *Social Action,* vol. 2(4), pp. 11-17.

Reed, B.G. (1985) Drug Misuse and Dependency in Women: The Meaning and Implications of Being Considered a Special Population or Minority Group, *The International Journal of the Addictions,* vol. 20(1), pp. 13-62.

Reed, B.G. (1987) Developing Women-sensitive Drug Dependence Treatment Services: Why So Difficult?, *Journal of Psychoactive Drugs,* vol. 19(2), pp. 151-164.

Rhoads, D.L. (1983) A Longitudinal Study of Life Stress and Social Support amongst Drug Abusers, *International Journal of Addiction,* vol. 18(2), pp. 195-222.

Riessman, C.K. (1992) Women and Medicalisation: A New Perspective, in Kirkup, G. and Smith Keller, L. (eds) *Inventing Women.* Polity Press, London.

Roberts, H. (1985) *The Patient Patients: Women and their Doctors.* Pandora Press, London.

Rohsenow, D. J., Corbett, R. and Devine, D. (1988) Molested as Children: A Hidden Contribution to Substance Abuse?, *Journal of Substance Abuse Treatment,* vol. 5, pp. 13-18.

Rosaldo, M.Z. and Lamphere, L. (1974) *Woman, Culture and Society.* Stanford University Press, Stanford, California.

Rosenbaum, M. (1981) Sex Roles Among Deviants: The Woman Addict, *International Journal of the Addictions,* vol. 16, pp. 859-877.

Rudestam, K.E. and Newton, R.R. (1992) *Surviving Your Dissertation: A Comprehensive Guide to Content and Process.* Sage Publications, London.

Sandmaier, M. (1980) *The Invisible Alcoholics.* McGraw-Hill Book Company, New York.

Sargent, M. (1992) *Women, Drugs and Policy in Sydney, London and Amsterdam.* Avebury, Aldershot.

Shephard, A. (1990) *Substance Dependency: A Professional Guide.* Venture Press Limited, Birmingham.

Simpson, T.L., Westerberg, V.S., Little, L.M., and Trujillo, M. (1994) Screening for Child Physical and Sexual Abuse among Outpatient Substance Abusers, *Journal of Substance Abuse Treatment*, vol. 11, pp. 347-358.

Sluka, J. A. (1989) Living on Their Nerves: Nervous Debility in Northern Ireland, in D.L. Davis and S. Low (eds) *Gender,Health and Illness: The Case of Nerves.* Hemisphere, New York.

Smart, C. (1984) Social Policy and Drug Addiction, *British Journal of Addiction*, vol. 79(1), pp. 31-9.

Smith, E.M., Cloninger, R. and Bradford, S. (1983) Predictors of Mortality in Alcoholic Women: A Prospective Follow-up Study, *Alcoholism: Clinical and Experimental Research*, vol. 7(2), pp. 237-243.

Smith, L.N. (1992a) A Descriptive Study of Alcohol-Dependent Women Attending Alcoholics Anonymous, A Regional Council on Alcoholism and an Alcohol Treatment Unit, *Alcohol and Alcoholism*, vol. 27(6), pp. 667-676.

Smith, L. N. (1992b) Help-Seeking in Alcohol Dependent Females, *Alcohol and Alcoholism*, vol. 27(1), pp. 3-9.

Stanko, E.A. (1985) *Intimate Intrusions: Women's Experiences of Male Violence.* Routledge and Kegan Paul, London.

Stanko, E.A. (1994) Dancing with Denial: Researching Women and Questioning Men, in M. Maynard and J. Purvis (eds) *Researching Women's Lives from a Feminist Perspective.* Taylor and Francis Ltd., London.

Strang, S. (1989) A Model Service, in S. MacGregor (ed.) *Drugs and British Society: Responses to a Social Problem in the Eighties.* Routledge, London.

Swift, W., Copeland, J. and Hall, W. (1996) Characteristics of Women with Alcohol and Other Drug Problems: Findings of an Australian National Survey, *Addiction*, vol. 91(8), pp. 1141-1150.

Taylor, A. (1993) *Women Drug Users.* Clarendon Press, Oxford.

Thom, B. (1984) A Process Approach to Women's Use of Alcohol Services, *British Journal of Addiction*, vol. 79, pp. 377-382.

Thom, B. (1986) Sex Differences in Help-Seeking for Alcohol Problems-1. The Barriers to Help-seeking, *British Journal of Addiction*, vol. 81, pp. 777-788

Thom, B. (1987) Sex Differences in Help-Seeking for Alcohol Problems - 2. Entry into Treatment, *British Journal of Addiction*, vol. 82, pp. 989-997.

Thom, B. (1994) Women and Alcohol: The Emergence of a Risk Group, in M. McDonald (ed.) *Gender, Drink and Drugs.* Berg, Oxford.

Thom, B. and Green, A. (1996) Services for Women: the Way Forward, in L. Harrison (ed.) *Alcohol Problems in the Community.* Routledge, London.

Thom, B. and Tellez, C. (1986) A Difficult Business: Detecting and Managing Problems in General Practice, *British Journal of Addiction*, vol. 81, pp. 405-418.

Ussher, J. (1991) *Women's Madness: Misogyny or Mental Illness.* Harvester Wheatsheaf, London.

Ussher, J. (1998) A Feminist Perspective, in R. Velleman, A. Copello and J. Maslin (eds) *Living With Drink: Women who Live with Problem Drinkers.* Longman, London.

Waller, T. (1993) *Drugs Work: Working with GPs.* ISDD, London.

Warren, C.A.B. (1988) *Gender Issues in Field Research.* Sage, London.

Waterson, J. (1996) Gender Divisions and Drinking Problems, in L. Harrison (ed.) *Alcohol Problems in the Community.* Routledge, London.

Williams, F. (1989) *Social Policy: A Critical Introduction.* Polity Press, Cambridge.

Wilsnack, S.C. and Wilsnack, R.W. (1991) Epidemiology of Women's Drinking, *Journal of Substance Abuse*, vol. 3, pp. 133-157.

Wister, A.V. and Avison, W.R. (1982) Friendly Persuasion: A Social Network Analysis of Sex Differences in Marijuana Use, *International Journal of the Addictions*, vol. 17, pp. 523-541.

Wolfson, D. and Murray, J. (eds) (1986) *Women and Dependency: Women's Personal Accounts of Drug and Alcohol Problems.* DAWN, London.

Women's National Commission (1988) *Stress and Addiction Amongst Women: Report of An Ad-Hoc Working Group.* London.

Young, E.B. (1990) The Role of Incest Issues in Relapse, *Journal of Psychoactive Drugs*, vol. 22(2), pp. 249-258.

Zanowski, G.L. (1987) Responsive Programming: Meeting the Needs of Chemically Dependent Women, *Alcoholism Treatment Quarterly*, vol. 4 (4), pp. 53-66.

Appendix 1: Research Design

Research Instruments

I chose to use predominantly qualitative measures for my study (although I also used brief questionnaires for collecting demographic details). This was primarily because the nature of the research problem, and the exploratory nature of the study appeared best served by a qualitative approach. As Jennifer Mason's (1996) working definition of qualitative research indicates, it is broadly associated with an interpretivist philosophical approach to social life, its methods of data collection are flexible, and it lends itself to producing 'rounded understandings' of participants' experiences; all of which characteristics were appropriate to the type of study I wished to conduct, and my own research ideology. The accounts and experiences related by women in the study reveal something of how they negotiated their experiences of alcohol and drug use in relation to other people, and the ideas, norms and beliefs within which they operate. This type of data would be difficult to obtain using primarily quantitative measures, for example questionnaires with a pre-set structure.

I therefore chose to use focus groups and semi-structured interviews as the main means of gathering data, supplemented by a field diary and brief questionnaires. There were particular aspects of this study, in addition to those previously mentioned, which guided my thinking in designing research instruments. The sensitive nature of the topic was a main consideration, for example:

> The research instrument has to be sensitive to the communication style and language of prospective respondents. If the instruments are not sensitive, respondents may not only misunderstand the questions, they may be offended by them and not give valid responses. (Bowser and Sieber, 1993, p167)

I was also concerned that the research should actually be meaningful to those taking part, and not based simply on my decisions about what should be included. In the initial phase of the research, therefore, a focus group, drawn from women resident in an alcohol treatment centre, was used to identify those issues of importance to participants. As Bowser and Sieber

137

(1993) suggest, this method is useful to ensure the research is actually able to 'measure something valid for subjects and will be an experience they can relate to' (p166). An important strength of the focus group resides in 'the explicit use of the group interaction to produce data and insights that would be less accessible without the interaction found in a group' (Morgan, 1988, p12). At an early stage of the research a focus group can provide access into the perspectives of the participants, suggest areas for study which might not be evident from the literature, and suggest topics to be further explored at the interview stage (Bowser and Sieber, 1993). In researching sensitive topics, such as drug and alcohol use, focus groups can provide a 'way in' to the subject for a researcher, and ensure that terms used throughout the research are in fact meaningful to participants, and not offensive to them.

The main part of the study consisted of semi-structured interviews using a topic sheet, based on the findings of the focus group, as an interview guide. However, this was not rigidly adhered to, as some areas of experience are obviously more important to certain individuals, depending on their personal history. A similar type of in-depth interview has been used in other studies of women with drug problems (see, for example, Sargent, 1992; Taylor, 1993). Following the suggestion of Morgan (1988) I also used direct quotations emerging from the focus group, to obtain individual reactions. The interviews were tape recorded, with permission, and lasted approximately one hour.

A brief questionnaire, including such topics as employment status, housing tenure and income, and number of children, was used in addition to the interviews. This type of research tool has been utilised, for example, by Adler and her colleagues (1993), in their study of female managers, and by Sargent (1992) as part of her study of drug users. Using questionnaires in this way allowed demographic details to be collected easily and quickly at the end of interviews. Interviews with senior personnel at alcohol and drugs agencies were also carried out using a questionnaire format.

A field diary was used, in addition to collecting substantive data, to note reflections on the research process as it progressed (cf. Rudestam and Newton, 1992). These were in the form of methodological notes, which are 'a record of the process of reflexivity, in which the researcher is included in the data' (Hugman, 1988, p14). Lynda Measor (1985) also suggests keeping a record of any feedback from participants of images of the self as researcher. When Taylor (1993) was conducting her research on the streets of Glasgow it was only a casual remark from a male drug user, overheard when the study was well underway, which alerted her to the extent to which she had been under scrutiny by those she was observing. Fortunately she had been accepted as an unthreatening presence. However, had the opposite been the case, her access to data might well have been restricted.

Sampling Strategy

Finding a sample of respondents when studying sensitive topics can be a problem, as Lee (1993) explains, 'the less visible an activity is, the harder it is to sample' (p60). Much drug use is 'hidden' in nature (and illegal). People with drug and alcohol problems are not readily identifiable, particularly those who do not seek treatment. This therefore affects sampling strategies available to drug and alcohol researchers. In common with Taylor's (1993) study of female heroin users my sample is not representative in any statistical sense; partly because the size of the problem alcohol and drug using population is inestimable, and partly because there is much hidden drug use.

When considering sampling strategies the aims of the research necessarily influence the choice of method. For example:

> Where the researcher's aim is to generate theory and a wider understanding of social processes or social actions, the representativeness of the sample may be of less importance and the best sampling strategy may be focused or judgmental sampling. (Arber, 1993, p71)

A judgmental sampling strategy relies on the researcher to seek out individuals with a range of different social characteristics or experiences (Hall and Hall, 1996). Taking into account the nature of the research project, which was primarily exploratory, and the lack of a ready sampling frame of women with alcohol and drug alcohol problems, I felt that this type of sampling method was most appropriate, and it was with that in mind that I began seeking participants. However, the practicalities of gaining access to a sample meant that I was effectively limited to those women attending treatment agencies.

Use of treatment agency clients as a population on which to draw is common in alcohol and drug research, as providing a ready pool of respondents, which is relatively easily accessible. This formed the basis of my research strategy; for example, the pilot study (consisting of a focus group and five individual interviews) took place in a hostel for female problem drinkers, while the main study was with female clients of voluntary and statutory alcohol and drug agencies. (I also attempted to make contact with women through local community groups, such as homeless hostels,

Alcoholics Anonymous and MIND, but this proved fruitless.) Agencies visited included both statutory and voluntary; residential and 'street' agencies. The sample was therefore as varied as possible under the constraints of the study.

Characteristics of Sample (see also Appendix 2)

Twenty-three women participated in the main study, seventeen of whom were resident in alcohol and drug rehabilitation units at the time; the remaining six in contact with community voluntary agencies. In addition, the views of ten senior agency staff from both the statutory and voluntary sector were sought. Women respondents were aged between twenty and forty-nine; the majority were white, one was black, and one Chinese (based on women's descriptions of their ethnic origins). Three women were living with their husbands immediately prior to entering treatment, and six with male partners (living arrangements with partners were, however, subject to frequent changes). Five women were living with parents (four of these had recent male partners), and five living alone. Thirteen women had dependent children; of these seven were lone parents (four living alone with children, three with parents).

The majority of women in the study (14) who gave details of their income were in receipt of less than £100 per week (net); six women received between £100 and £150 per week; and one between £150 to £200 per week. Ten women were local authority tenants, five were tenants in the private sector, six were owner occupiers, and two lived with parents.

The women's primary drug of use is categorised as follows: alcohol ($n=15$) ; heroin ($n=6$) ; amphetamines ($n=2$). Illegal drug users tend to be younger, have more chaotic lifestyles and condensed careers of drug use; that is the development of health, social and financial problems occurred more quickly than for women using alcohol as the main substance of choice. (N.B. I have categorised the women's primary drug of use as the substance which brought them into contact with alcohol and drug agencies.)

However there is some overlap between the groups; three women who drank also used illegal drugs, for example. This latter group has characteristics in common with women whose primary drug of use was heroin or amphetamines, in terms of age (aged 35 and under, average age 27) and lifestyle, whereas women with alcohol problems were generally aged in their thirties or forties (average age 43) ($n=12$). Women using a combination of alcohol and drugs are therefore included with heroin and amphetamine users for the purposes of analysis (*n*=11).

The sample includes women from a variety of family backgrounds, a wide age range, varied employment histories, different living arrangements, and with differing 'careers' of alcohol and drug dependency. Despite having in common contact with treatment agencies, the sample is therefore wide ranging in terms of the participants' characteristics. The findings of the study are indicative, however, rather than representative.

Ethical Issues

Studying topics which are potentially threatening to the individual poses particular problems of ethics to the social researcher, in addition to those of concern to feminist researchers in general. For example:

> Telling another about those aspects of one's self which are in some way intimate or personally discrediting - confessing in other words - is a difficult business. It becomes less so where privacy and anonymity are guaranteed and when disclosure takes place in a non-censorious atmosphere. (Lee, 1993, p97)

Areas of particular concern in this study were those of informed consent and the need to protect participants from harm (Rudestam and Newton, 1992). As O'Connell Davidson and Layder (1994) point out, where research involves groups who are relatively powerless informed consent needs to be carefully addressed, to avoid exploiting those taking part. This is particularly the case with a 'captive' research group, for example, in an institutional setting, where people may feel a sense of obligation to take part. In a group situation confidentiality within the group is also an issue which needs to be specifically addressed.

Explanatory handouts were therefore provided for potential participants, detailing the aims of the research, the reasons why they were being asked to participate, the length of time the interview or group was likely to take, and my background as a researcher. It was made clear that participation was voluntary and could be terminated at any time, and that any questions which were unacceptable to respondents need not be answered. Issues of confidentiality, anonymity and possible uses of the data were also explained. Women were invited to choose a pseudonym for use in the research report. Questions were also invited from participants before consent was formally obtained and the focus group or interview began (Rudestam and Newton,

1992). When the questionnaires were completed at the end of interviews it was also stressed that the material was confidential, and that no names would be attached to them.

As Lee (1993) points out, research participants may not always realise, in advance of interviews, the true implications of what research may involve, and potential risks to themselves. Obtaining consent is therefore not a once and for all event. The researcher needs to be aware of problems arising for participants during research, for example concerning disclosure of distressing experiences, or events damaging to their self image. By remaining sensitive to the needs of participants these negative aspects can be minimised. Debriefing after the focus group and interviews provided an opportunity to assess the type of experience it had been for the participants, clear up any misconceptions regarding the research, and offer follow up support where possible.

Research Procedures

This section describes how participants in the study were contacted, the methods used to obtain co-operation, and how the research instruments were applied in practice.

Pilot Study

Turning Point at Manchester was selected as the site for the pilot study, partly because it was known that they had previously invited researchers into their agency, and partly because the location, outside Cumbria, would not interfere with obtaining the sample for the main study. Turning Point is a charitable organisation, providing services for people with drug, alcohol, and mental health problems. In Manchester the facilities include a women's rehabilitation hostel, which was for me the main point of interest; and the Smithfield Centre, which offers a drop-in, telephone advice, detoxification facilities, group and individual support and social and recreational activities.

The initial approach was made to the area manager of Turning Point, in a letter explaining the nature of the pilot study in broad terms. The reply was favourable, and asked for more details, for consideration by staff and clients of the project. When this was forwarded and accepted, a telephone contact was made with the team leader at the women's hostel to arrange an initial visit. This was to include a focus group conducted at the hostel, followed by observation of the women's drop-in at the Smithfield Centre.

After verbal and written explanations to those involved, and a brief icebreaker, a focus group discussion took place involving six female residents, which I led with the aid of a topic sheet. One of the problems with conducting a focus group is finding a balance as a facilitator between allowing the discussion to diversify to the extent that it is no longer relevant to the research objectives, and not being directive to the extent that the facilitator dominates the discussion. Finally, it depends on the purpose of the group, the skills of the facilitator, and the use to which the data will be put. For my own purposes I elicited some useful data, but I had to think quickly and discard some preplanned questions, as they were obviously irrelevant, or would have jarred in that context. The discussion lasted approximately fifty minutes and was tape recorded with the agreement of all the women present. Time was allotted at the end of the group for a debriefing and an informal talk. Whenever the opportunity arose throughout my visit to the hostel I also took part in the social activities, which consisted mainly of drinking coffee and talking.

A room was provided at the hostel, where I was able to write up notes on issues arising from the focus group, while they were still fresh in my mind. The women's shared space did not seem an appropriate place to do this, as I did not wish to appear overly intrusive. Nor did I wish to cause anxiety amongst the women concerning what I might be writing.

I returned to the hostel for a two day visit to conduct individual interviews. I arrived at the conclusion of the regular morning group meeting, introduced myself to the group and again explained the purpose of my research. I asked for volunteers to be interviewed and five women came forward (from a total of seven present). These included two of the original residents who had taken part in the focus group. Because of changes in clientele between the two visits explanations of the purpose of the research were again necessary.

I issued a handout to each participant at the beginning of each interview, explaining their involvement. Pseudonyms were also agreed with participants, as an aid to anonymity. An interview schedule, developed from the focus group discussion, was used as an interview guide. However, this was not rigidly adhered to, as some areas of experience are obviously more important to certain individuals, depending on their personal history. Following the suggestion of Morgan (1988) I also used direct quotations emerging from the focus group, to obtain individual reactions. The interviews were tape recorded, with permission, and lasted approximately one hour. Immediately following the interviews the women completed a brief questionnaire, providing demographic details. This took only a few minutes to complete and presented few problems. Finally, a short debriefing was carried out. Field notes were written up as soon as practicable.

Answering questions about myself was something which arose throughout the interviews. I decided that as the women were offering me personal information it was only fair to reciprocate. Two of the women, one of whom had recently studied for a degree, expressed an interest in the details of my research.

The interviews took place over a two day period, as far as possible fitting in with the normal running of the hostel. Prior to leaving I agreed to provide Turning Point with a brief report on the results of my visit, as a form of feedback.

Main Study

The main period of data collection was from December 1996 to July 1997. Initially I made contact with voluntary agencies, as at that stage I was still in the process of negotiating approval from the appropriate Medical Ethics Committee. My first contact was eased by my previous experience as a volunteer with the agency in question, and having done a small research project for them as an undergraduate. My credentials as a researcher were therefore at least partially established. In addition a women's support group was in existence at the agency. I was able, therefore, with the prior agreement of the women concerned, to visit the group, explain the research, and make arrangements for individual interviews. Eventually I carried out two interviews on agency premises and two in women's homes, in addition to interviewing the agency manager. A further contact with another voluntary agency was also successful in producing two participants.

After what appeared to be a fairly promising beginning, however, subsequent interviews were to prove somewhat more difficult to arrange. Visits to one rehabilitation unit in the voluntary sector were accomplished through a contact on the Drug Reference Group, of which I was then a member. Prior to visiting this agency, and another voluntary sector drug rehabilitation unit, extensive contacts with senior staff were necessary, initially by letter, followed by telephone calls. However, after one successful visit, the agency managers were happy to arrange further contacts with their clients.

At this stage of the research, having carried out several interviews in voluntary agencies, I was then able to contact staff from statutory alcohol and drug agencies in the Morecambe Bay area. The most fruitful contact in this part of the study was with an alcohol rehabilitation unit, where I was able to arrange a number of interviews over a period of some months. Subsequent visits to agencies were often worthwhile, as they had often received new clients in the intervening period. Residential agencies were to prove the main source of study participants, as reflected in the composition of my final sample; seventeen of whom were in residential rehabilitation at the time of the study. Approaches to community alcohol and drug teams, although staff were willing to be interviewed personally, and pass on introductory letters to their clients (except for one outright refusal), brought no contacts. In two cases team leaders were particularly enthusiastic about the research, and optimistic about finding participants, but to no avail.

The difficulties experienced in finding a sample underline the problems inherent in this type of research. Without my existing local knowledge and prior contacts the process could have been even more problematic. Persistence was usually rewarded with one or two fresh contacts, but not invariably so. I was puzzled (and remain so) by the reluctance of clients of statutory community alcohol and drug teams to take part in the research, and the staff concerned could offer no explanations. I can only attribute this reluctance to alcohol and drug users' natural wariness of researchers, and the lack of first-hand contacts with women in touch with statutory community agencies (although with voluntary agencies such approaches were more successful). Working through an intermediary, where direct contacts with potential participants are not possible, does increase the difficulties for the researcher in overcoming initial barriers of mistrust and suspicion. The majority of women with whom I had direct contact, either through the women's group or through rehabilitation agencies, readily agreed to take part in the research, and a number appeared actively to enjoy the experience.

Appendix 2: Characteristics of Sample

Table 1 Study Participants: primary substance of use

Substance Type	Pilot Study Group	Pilot Study Interviews	Main Study Interviews
Alcohol	6	5	12
Alcohol / drugs			3
Heroin			6
Amphetamine			2
Total	6	5	23